| 汉英对照 |

中国军事关键词

KEYWORDS TO UNDERSTAND CHINA

National Defense and Military Development

中国外文出版发行事业局（CIPG）
当代中国与世界研究院（ACCWS）
中国翻译研究院（CATL）

新世界出版社
NEW WORLD PRESS

First Edition 2021

Compiled by
China International Publishing Group
Academy of Contemporary China and World Studies
China Academy of Translation

Translated by
Cai Lijian

English text edited by
David Ferguson,
Han Qingyue
and Xu Mingqiang

Cover designed by
He Yuting

ISBN 978-7-5104-7234-3

Published by
NEW WORLD PRESS
24 Baiwanzhuang Street, Beijing 100037, China

Distributed by
NEW WORLD PRESS
24 Baiwanzhuang Street, Beijing 100037, China
Tel: 86-10-68995968
Fax: 86-10-68998705
Website: www.nwp.com.cn
E-mail: nwpcd@sina.com

Printed in the People's Republic of China

《中国关键词》
图书编委会

《中国军事关键词》图书编辑人员

中文编写人员：

安　平　葛立德　关　泠
姜铁军　刘光明　马德宝
马　刚　孟祥青　苗润奇
任　剑　尚　伟　王长勤
王　强　吴志忠　徐　辉
于　淼　曾华锋　张军社
赵晓冬　周俊杰

中文咨询人员：

陈明明　丁　刚　丁　洁
贾　永　申　阳　汪守德
王刚毅　徐亚男　杨　平
于运全　张　锋　朱鸿亮

英文翻译、编辑组：

蔡力坚　David Ferguson［英］
韩清月　徐明强

Keywords to Understand China: National Defense and Military Development

Editorial Team

Editors (Chinese Text):

An Ping, Ge Lide, Guan Ling,
Jiang Tiejun, Liu Guangming, Ma Debao,
Ma Gang, Meng Xiangqing, Miao Runqi,
Ren Jian, Shang Wei, Wang Changqin,
Wang Qiang, Wu Zhizhong, Xu Hui,
Yu Miao, Zeng Huafeng, Zhang Junshe,
Zhao Xiaodong, Zhou Junjie

Consultants (Chinese Text):

Chen Mingming, Ding Gang, Ding Jie,
Jia Yong, Shen Yang, Wang Shoude,
Wang Gangyi, Xu Yanan, Yang Ping,
Yu Yunquan, Zhang Feng, Zhu Hongliang

Editors (English Text):

Cai Lijian, David Ferguson (UK),
Han Qingyue, Xu Mingqiang

前 言

新时代中国国防和军队建设取得历史性成就、发生历史性变革，中国军队在世界舞台上发挥着越来越重要的作用，日益受到国际社会聚焦关注。中国始终是世界和平的建设者、全球发展的贡献者、国际秩序的维护者，中国军队始终是维护世界和平的坚定力量。

读懂中国军队，既需要从整体面貌上观察，也需要点击关键词、从不同侧面加深了解。为此，我们组织编写了《中国军事关键词》，主要围绕习近平强军思想、中国国防政策和军事理念、新时代强军实践，选取了 77 个具有标志性、代表性的关键词，进行中文词条释义，并翻译成英语、法语、俄语、西班牙语、阿拉伯语、德语、葡语、意大利语、日语、韩语、越南语、印尼语、土耳其语、哈萨克语等 14 个语种，通过平面、网络和移动社交平台等多媒体、多渠道、多形态对外发布，阐释中国军事思想和军事理念，解读中国国防政策和中国特色强军之路。

我们深知，仅用几十个关键词，很难涵盖习近平强军思想的丰富内容，很难将中国国防和军队建设故事讲全面、讲清楚、讲完整，也很难全景式呈现新时代强军事业的立体画面，我们的全部努力在于，为读者提供一把感知、了解、认识、读懂中国国防和军队建设的钥匙。

由于能力及时间所限，在中文词条遴选编写时，难免挂一漏万。本书为中外文对照版，为使译文更符合目标语读者的阅读习惯，我们对传统的两种语言“高度一致性”原则作了创新探索，旨在提升读者的阅读体验，译文表达难免有不贴切之处、不尽如人意之处，我们真诚地欢迎大家提出宝贵的意见建议。书中有关数据如无特殊说明，统计截止时间均为 2020 年 9 月。

点击中国军事关键词，链接东方军事文明，走进新时代的中国军队。让大量客观事实见证：服务构建人类命运共同体，中国军队一直在努力。

Introduction

The advent of a new era has heralded changes and new achievements in China's national defense and military development. The role of China's armed forces is growing in importance in the world arena and attracting more attention from around the world. China will stay committed as ever to maintaining world peace, contributing to global prosperity, and upholding the international order, and the Chinese military will remain as always a firm force in defending world peace.

To understand China's military, it is important to view it from a range of perspectives and obtain a full picture. Equally important is to understand a number of key concepts. This series of keywords explains Xi Jinping thought on strengthening the military, China's national defense policy and military doctrine, and how the policy and doctrine are applied in the new era.

This booklet contains 77 keywords touching upon a broad range of issues concerning China's national defense. Compiled in Chinese, these keywords have been translated into 14 other languages – Arabic, English, French, German, Indonesian Bahasa, Italian, Japanese, Kazakh, Korean, Portuguese, Russian, Spanish, Turkish and Vietnamese. They are also available online and can be accessed on social media platforms. We hope that this new series will help international audience build a better understanding of China's defense landscape.

We know that explaining a few dozen key concepts cannot do justice to the extent of Xi Jinping thought on strengthening the military, and to China's ongoing efforts to strengthen national defense in the new era. Our goal here is to present to our audience the broadest possible picture of development in China's defense capability in the fewest possible words.

Due to the scope of the project and its tight schedule, oversights and inaccuracies are possible in our selection of entries. Its foreign language versions may not correspond exactly to the Chinese text at the word level, as intrinsic differences between languages and the need for a certain degree of target audience orientation effectively render any attempt at establishing word-level equivalence unhelpful. A new approach has been adopted to achieve the optimal level of textual equivalence. We welcome any comments and suggestions for future improvements. Unless otherwise specified, all statistics contained herein represent the situation as of September 2020.

"Keywords to Understand China: National Defense and Military Development" can be read online, together with additional information about new development of China's military in the new era, and about how it serves the goal of building a global community with a shared future.

Contents
目 录

中国军事关键词

Keywords to Understand China: National Defense and Military Development

习近平强军思想

习近平强军思想，是习近平新时代中国特色社会主义思想的重要组成部分，是中国共产党军事指导理论的最新成果，是坚持走中国特色强军之路、全面推进国防和军队现代化的行动纲领。

中国共产党第十八次全国代表大会以来，以习近平同志为核心的党中央，着眼于实现中华民族伟大复兴的中国梦，围绕新时代建设一支什么样的强大人民军队、怎样建设强大人民军队，带领全军深入进行理论探索和实践创造，形成了习近平强军思想。在中国共产党第十九次全国代表大会后军队一次重要会议上，习近平阐述了“十个明确”。这“十个明确”涵盖新时代军队建设、改革和军事斗争准备各领域各方面，构成了习近平强军思想的主要内容。2019年5月，中央军委政治工作部印

Xi Jinping Thought on Strengthening the Military

Xi Jinping thought on strengthening the military is an important part of Xi Jinping Thought on Socialism with Chinese Characteristics for a New Era. It represents the latest development of the military philosophy of the Communist Party of China (CPC), and provides a guideline for a unique Chinese approach to strengthening national defense and building a strong, modern military.

Since the 18th CPC National Congress held in November 2012, the Central Committee with Xi Jinping at its core has been making theoretical and practical efforts to identify what kind of military to be built in order to respond to the new realities in the new era and help make the great Chinese Dream of national renewal come true, and what steps should be taken to build such a military. The outcome of these discussions has come to be known as Xi Jinping thought on strengthening the military, the main pillars of which embody the "Ten-point Guidelines" illustrated by Xi at an important meeting on military affairs after the 19th CPC National Congress. These guidelines emphasize the need for further development and reform of the military in the new era to step up its military preparedness in various aspects.

发《习近平强军思想学习纲要》，围绕强国必须强军，建设一支听党指挥、能打胜仗、作风优良的人民军队，坚持党对人民军队的绝对领导，抓思想政治建设一刻也不能放松，与时俱进创新军事战略指导，军队要能打仗、打胜仗，掌握强军打赢的科学方法论，改革是决定我军发展壮大、制胜未来的关键一招，建设创新型人民军队，提高国防和军队建设法治化水平，建设强大的现代化后勤，把武器装备建设搞得更好一些、更快一些，构建一体化的国家战略体系和能力，全面加强新时代军队党的建设，努力培养造就能够担当强军重任的高素质干部和人才队伍，坚定不移正风肃纪、反腐惩恶等重大思想观点进行了全面阐释。

习近平强军思想，引领中国国防和军队建设取得历史性成就、发生历史性变革，把中国共产党对国防和军队建设规律、军事斗争准备规律、战争指导规律的认识提升到新高度，开拓了当代中国马克

In May 2019, the Political Work Department of the Central Military Commission (CMC) issued a study guide designed to foster the understanding of Xi Jinping thought on strengthening the military, which calls for:

- building a people's military that obeys the Party's command, is able to fight and win, and maintains excellent conduct;
- upholding the Party's absolute leadership over the military;
- strengthening political awareness;
- encouraging new thinking and developing sound strategies to ensure that the military is able to win wars;
- pursuing reform and encouraging innovation, which are key to its strength;
- strengthening law-based governance;
- improving modern logistic service;
- upgrading weaponry and equipment;
- bolstering integrated strategic capabilities;
- strengthening the Party development within the armed forces;
- enhancing military leadership development and talent building; and
- enforcing ethics and discipline, and stamping out corruption.

Xi Jinping thought on strengthening the military guides our efforts to strengthen national defense and the military with impressive results and profound changes unprecedented in history. It provides a new understanding of how the CPC should best play its role in this area, including how to

思主义军事理论和军事实践发展新境界。2017年10月，中国共产党第十九次全国代表大会确立了习近平强军思想在国防和军队建设中的指导地位，并将其写入中国共产党党章。

improve military preparedness and update its war doctrine, and raise China's Marxist military theory to new heights.

At the 19th National Congress in October 2017, the CPC decided to write Xi Jinping thought on strengthening the military in the CPC Constitution as the guiding principle for defense and military development.

国防和军队建设进入新时代

2017年10月18日，中国共产党召开第十九次全国代表大会，习近平向大会作了题为《决胜全面建成小康社会　夺取新时代中国特色社会主义伟大胜利》的报告，指出“中国特色社会主义进入了新时代”，这是对中国发展历史方位的全新界定。2017年10月26日，习近平在军队领导干部会议上指出，中国特色社会主义进入了新时代，国防和军队建设也进入了新时代。这是对中国国防和军队建设所处历史方位的战略判断，意味着人民军队内外环境有了新变化、使命任务有了新拓展、建设发展有了新要求。

China's Defense and Military Development Enters the New Era

In his report "Secure a Decisive Victory in Building a Moderately Prosperous Society in All Respects and Strive for the Great Success of Socialism with Chinese Characteristics for a New Era" delivered at the 19th CPC National Congress on October 18, 2017, Xi Jinping declared that China had entered a new era of socialism with Chinese characteristics, opening a new chapter in the Chinese history.

At a meeting of senior military leaders on October 26, 2017, he further pointed out that a new era for China's socialism also meant a new era for China's national defense and armed forces, offering a strategic vision for China's new defense needs that sets new requirements for the mission of the military and its future trajectory in response to domestic and global changes.

党在新时代的强军目标

习近平着眼实现中华民族伟大复兴中国梦提出新时代军队建设目标。

在各个历史时期，中国共产党都根据形势任务的变化，明确提出人民军队建设发展的目标要求，引领军队建设不断向前发展。2013年3月11日，习近平在十二届全国人大一次会议解放军代表团全体会议上，将建设一支听党指挥、能打胜仗、作风优良的人民军队确立为强军目标。2017年10月18日，习近平在中国共产党第十九次全国代表大会的报告中指出，党在新时代的强军目标是建设一支听党指挥、能打胜仗、作风优良的人民军队，把人民军队建设成为世界一流军队。听党指挥是灵魂，决定军队建设的政治方向；能打胜仗是核心，反映军队的根本职能和军队建设的根本指向；作风优良是保证，关系军队的性质、宗旨、本色。到本世纪中叶，把人民军队全面建成世界一流军队，这就是

The Party's Goal of Building a Strong Military in the New Era

Xi Jinping frames the goal of building a strong military in the new era as part of his vision for realizing the Chinese Dream of national renewal.

The CPC has succeeded in guiding the people's armed forces through various historical periods by setting new requirements for their missions in response to a changing context.

Addressing the plenary meeting of the People's Liberation Army (PLA) delegates to the first session of the 12th National People's Congress (NPC) on March 11, 2013, Xi Jinping outlined the goal of building a people's military that obeys the Party's command, is able to fight and win, and maintains excellent conduct.

He reaffirmed this imperative in his report to the Party's 19th National Congress, and added that we should build the people's forces into world-class forces. Specifically, he emphasized the importance of the Party's absolute leadership over the military, which is the soul of the military and determines its political direction, the need to improve its combat capabilities which is its fundamental function, and the need to strengthen discipline and ethics so as to ensure that it stays true to

建成同我国强国地位相称、能够全面有效维护国家安全、具备强大国际影响力的世界一流军队。

its nature, purpose and character. The goal is to create a world-class military capable of effectively defending the national security and exerting global influence by the mid-21st century, coinciding with China's effort to build a strong country.

中国特色强军之路

坚持走中国特色强军之路，是新时代中国国防的发展路径。

中国特色强军之路，本质特征是坚持中国共产党对人民军队的绝对领导，坚持人民军队的性质、宗旨、本色。基本要求是深入贯彻习近平强军思想，坚持政治建军、改革强军、科技强军、人才强军、依法治军，聚焦能打仗、打胜仗，推动机械化信息化融合发展，加快军事智能化发展，构建中国特色现代军事力量体系，完善和发展中国特色社会主义军事制度，不断提高履行新时代使命任务能力。战略目标是把人民军队全面建成世界一流军队。

The Chinese Path of Building Strong Armed Forces

China is applying its own unique approach to developing the military in the new era.

China's unique approach to strengthening the military calls for the CPC's absolute leadership over the people's armed forces, which adhere to its nature, purpose and character.

It is essential to implement Xi Jinping thought on strengthening the military, raise political awareness, proceed with necessary reform, develop science and technology, build talent, and improve law-based governance. Also critical are measures to enhance the capabilities to win wars and perform the missions in the new era by leveraging new technologies, integrate mechanization and informationization, speed up development of intelligent military, build a unique modern military force structure, and improve the military system with Chinese features. China's strategic goal is to develop a world-class military.

政治建军、改革强军、科技强军、人才强军、依法治军

2019年12月，习近平在军队一次重要会议上提出，坚持政治建军、改革强军、科技强军、人才强军、依法治军。政治建军主要是发挥政治工作生命线作用，确保党对人民军队的绝对领导，永葆人民军队性质、宗旨、本色。改革强军主要是解决制约国防和军队建设的体制性障碍、结构性矛盾、政策性问题，推进军队组织形态现代化，构建中国特色现代军事力量体系，完善和发展中国特色社会主义军事制度。科技强军主要是树立科技是核心战斗力的思想，坚持自主创新的战略基点，提高科技创新对人民军队建设和战斗力发展的贡献率。人才强军主要是把培养干部、培养人才摆在更加突出的位置，着力

Enhancing Political Awareness, Reform, Science and Technology, Talent Development, and Law-Based Governance

Addressing an important meeting in December 2019, Xi Jinping emphasized the need to enhance the political loyalty of the armed forces, strengthen the military through reform and technology, train high-caliber military personnel, and run the military in accordance with law.

Raising political awareness is essential to ensuring the Party's absolute leadership role and the military's continued adherence to its nature, purpose, and character.

Reform is key to addressing institutional, structural and organizational constraints in order to create a modern military force structure and an updated military system with Chinese features that serves China's socialist development.

Investing in new technologies means investing in force multipliers. A strategic focus on innovation ensures an increased role of science and technology in the effort to strengthen the military, especially its combat capabilities.

It is important to strengthen talent

锻造忠诚干净担当的高素质干部队伍，着力集聚矢志强军打赢的各方面优秀人才。依法治军主要是构建完善中国特色军事法治体系，推动治军方式根本性转变，提高国防和军队建设法治化水平。

management and build a strong team of military leaders and other professionals able to perform their duties with competence, integrity, dependability, and courage.

The goal of improving law-based governance in the military is to build a military legal system with Chinese features, bring about fundamental transformation in how the military is run, and enforce laws and rules effectively.

新时代军队使命任务

2017年12月，习近平在军队一次重要会议上指出，人民军队必须服从服务于党的历史使命，把握新时代国家安全战略需求，担当起党和人民赋予的新时代使命任务。2019年7月24日，国务院新闻办公室发表《新时代的中国国防》白皮书明确指出：进入新时代，中国军队依据国家安全和发展战略要求,坚决履行党和人民赋予的使命任务，为巩固中国共产党领导和社会主义制度提供战略支撑，为捍卫国家主权、统一、领土完整提供战略支撑，为维护国家海外利益提供战略支撑，为促进世界和平与发展提供战略支撑。

Missions and Tasks of China's Armed Forces in the New Era

At a meeting of military leaders in December 2017, Xi Jinping highlighted the responsibility of the armed forces to implement the Party's mission in response to new security and strategic challenges in the new era.

The white paper *China's National Defense in the New Era* issued by the State Council Information Office on July 24, 2019, explains:

In the new era, to meet the strategic demands of national security and development, China's armed forces firmly implement the missions and tasks entrusted by the CPC and the people. They endeavor to provide strategic support for consolidating the leadership of the CPC and the socialist system, safeguarding national sovereignty, unity, and territorial integrity, protecting China's overseas interests, and promoting world peace and development.

新时代军事战略方针

军事战略方针是军事力量建设与运用的总方略，并随着时代发展充实完善。新中国成立以来，人民军队继承积极防御战略思想和战略传统，先后对军事战略方针进行了8次重大调整，平均8—10年调整一次。

习近平亲自主持制定的新时代军事战略方针，于2019年1月颁布出台。新时代军事战略方针，坚持防御、自卫、后发制人原则，实行积极防御，坚持“人不犯我、我不犯人，人若犯我、我必犯人”，强调遏制战争与打赢战争相统一，强调战略上防御与战役战斗上进攻相统一。

Military Strategic Guideline for a New Era

Military strategy guides the development and employment of military forces. It is constantly updated and improved in response to the changing realities. Since the founding of the People's Republic of China in 1949, the people's armed forces have pursued a military strategy featuring active defense, which has undergone eight major adjustments, roughly once every eight to ten years.

Xi Jinping personally presided over the formulation of the military strategic guideline for a new era, which was unveiled in January 2019. The updated military strategy reiterates the principle of self-defense, that is, the use of military force only for defensive purposes. "We will not attack unless we are attacked; if we are attacked, we will certainly counterattack." China's military strategy aims to deter wars in addition to ensuring its ability to win wars. It focuses on a defensive posture complemented by effective offensive capabilities.

建设创新型人民军队

2017年10月18日，习近平在中国共产党第十九次全国代表大会的报告中提出，建设创新型人民军队。建设创新型人民军队，要求把创新摆在更加突出的位置，坚持向科技创新要战斗力，统筹推进军事理论、技术、组织、管理、文化等各方面创新，把人民军队建设模式和战斗力生成模式转到创新驱动发展轨道上来，推动国防和军队建设实现新跨越。建设创新型人民军队，顺应了世界科技革命、产业革命、军事革命发展趋势，体现了对现代战争规律、军队建设规律的科学把握，对推进强军事业具有重要意义。

An Innovative Approach to Building the People's Armed Forces

In his report to the 19th CPC National Congress, Xi Jinping called for an innovative approach to building the people's armed forces.

This approach underscores the increased importance of innovation and requires expanded use of new technologies in enhancing the military's combat capabilities. It also requires an integrated push to develop innovative military doctrine, organizational and governance practices, technology and culture, in order to remake the military and substantially upgrade its combat capabilities through an innovation-driven process. The move to reinvent China's armed forces responds to global technology trends, including trends in the new industrial revolution, especially those related to military technology. It is based on a sound understanding of modern warfare and defense imperatives, and will prove critical to efforts in this regard.

国防和军队现代化“三步走”战略安排

2017年10月18日，习近平在中国共产党第十九次全国代表大会的报告中提出：适应世界新军事革命发展趋势和国家安全需求，提高建设质量和效益，确保到2020年基本实现机械化，信息化建设取得重大进展，战略能力有大的提升。同国家现代化进程相一致，全面推进军事理论现代化、军队组织形态现代化、军事人员现代化、武器装备现代化，力争到2035年基本实现国防和军队现代化，到本世纪中叶把人民军队全面建成世界一流军队。

Three Steps to Modernize China's National Defense and Military in the New Era

In his report to the 19th CPC National Congress, Xi Jinping outlined a three-step plan for China's military modernization.

As the first step, the plan aims to achieve substantial progress by 2020 in improving the quality and efficiency of the military services and upgrading their combat capabilities – this in response to new global military technology trends and new national security needs – especially through the expanded use of mechanization and informationization solutions.

The second step calls for basic modernization of China's national defense and military services by 2035 through modernizing military theory, organizational structure, service personnel, and weaponry.

The final step will be the transformation of China's military into a world-class military by the mid-21st century.

国防和军队建设“四个现代化”

2017年10月18日，习近平在中国共产党第十九次全国代表大会的报告中提出，同国家现代化进程相一致，全面推进军事理论现代化、军队组织形态现代化、军事人员现代化、武器装备现代化。军事理论现代化，就是大力推进马克思主义军事理论创新，加快形成具有时代性、引领性、独特性的军事理论体系。军队组织形态现代化，就是深化国防和军队改革，推进军事管理革命，构建符合规律的科学制度机制。军事人员现代化，就是加强军事人才培养体系建设，大力培养联合作战指挥人才、新型作战力量人才、高层次科技创新人才、高水平战略管理人才，打造宏大的高素质新型军事人才队伍。武器装备

A Four-Pronged Initiative to Modernize China's National Defense and Military

In his report to the 19th CPC National Congress, Xi Jinping called for an all-round push to modernize military theory, military organizational structure, service personnel, and weaponry, in sync with the nation's economic modernization.

Modernizing military theory entails innovative development of Marxist military theory and creation of a unique theoretical framework that examines all aspects of war in a contemporary context and guides action to address any related challenges.

Organizational modernization aims to bring about changes in governance practices and align these practices with well-defined objectives.

Service personnel modernization requires enhanced measures for developing military talent to build a team of high-caliber military personnel, including joint operations commanders and specialists on new-type combat forces, technological innovation, and strategic management.

To modernize weaponry and equipment, it is critical to enhance combat capabilities through technological innovation and speed

现代化，就是坚持向科技创新要战斗力，加快发展高新技术武器装备，尽快建成适应现代战争和履行使命要求的武器装备体系。

up the development of high-tech weaponry and equipment that will prove effective in modern warfare and the efforts by the military to perform its duties.

坚持党对人民军队的绝对领导

坚持党对人民军队的绝对领导，就是全军对党要绝对忠诚，军队必须完全地、无条件地置于中国共产党的领导之下。坚持党对人民军队的绝对领导是中国特色社会主义的本质特征，是党和国家的重要政治优势，是人民军队的建军之本、强军之魂。

中国共产党缔造和领导的人民军队，从初创时期就确立了党指挥枪的原则。党对人民军队的绝对领导的根本原则和制度，发端于南昌起义、奠基于三湾改编、定型于古田会议，经过长期发展日臻完善，形成了包括坚持军队最高领导权和指挥权属于党中央、中央军委，中央军委实行主席负责制，实行党委制、政治委员制、政治机关制，实行党委统一的集体领导下的首长分工负责制，实行支部建在连

The CPC's Absolute Leadership over the People's Armed Forces

Ensuring the Party's absolute leadership over the military means ensuring that the military always remains absolutely loyal to the Party, and is completely and unconditionally placed under the Party's leadership. The Party's leadership over the military is a fundamental characteristic of Chinese socialism. It represents one of the greatest strengths of the Party and the nation, and underpins an effort to build a strong military.

The people's armed forces were created by the Party. Ever since its founding, it has been under the Party's leadership. The principle of the Party's leadership over the military originated from the Nanchang Uprising in 1927, developed during the Sanwan Reorganization of the same year, and was confirmed at the Gutian Meeting in 1929.

It has been enriched over the long years and developed into an institutional framework which ensures that the command and control of the armed forces resides with the CPC Central Committee and the CMC – the latter is under the direction of its chairperson. It is implemented through Party committees, political commissars, and specialized political staff in the military. It requires the presence

上等在内的一整套制度体系。中国共产党第十九次全国代表大会把坚持党对人民军队的绝对领导确定为新时代坚持和发展中国特色社会主义的基本方略。

of Party organizations in each military unit at or above the company level to ensure the Party's leadership, which is exercised by Party committees through a collective decision-making process.

At its 19th National Congress, the CPC reiterated the Party's absolute leadership over the military as fundamental for developing socialism with Chinese characteristics in the new era.

军委主席负责制

军委主席负责制是坚持党对人民军队的绝对领导的根本制度和根本实现形式，是中国共产党在实践中探索建立的党和国家相统一的最高军事领导体制，是中国特色社会主义政治制度和军事制度的重要组成部分。

1982年《中华人民共和国宪法》规定，“中央军事委员会实行主席负责制”。2017年10月，中国共产党第十九次全国代表大会决定，把“中央军事委员会实行主席负责制”写入《中国共产党章程》。军委主席负责制关系人民军队最高领导权和指挥权，在中国共产党领导军队的一整套制度体系中处于最高层次、居于统领地位。其基本内涵主要包括：中央军委主席负责中央军委全面工作；中央军委主席领导指挥全国武装力量；中央军委主席决定国防

The CMC Chairperson Responsibility System

The CMC chairperson responsibility system is the institutional arrangement for practicing the Party's absolute leadership over the military. It represents the top of the military chain of command, a role that combines central direction functions of both the Party and the state. This assignment of responsibility is based on experience the Party has gained, and constitutes an important element of China's socialist political and military systems.

The Constitution of the People's Republic of China (1982) stipulates, "The Central Military Commission shall practice a chairperson responsibility system." At its 19th National Congress in October 2017, the CPC decided to enshrine in the CPC Constitution that "Chairperson of the Central Military Commission assumes overall responsibility over the work of the commission." This rule vests the supreme military decision-making power in the chairperson of the CMC, and places this position at the very top of the organizational hierarchy of the people's armed forces under the leadership of the CPC. It stipulates that the chairperson of the CMC gives overall direction for the work of the commission, commands the armed forces, and makes decisions on all major issues

和军队建设一切重大问题。

人民军队必须全面深入贯彻军委主席负责制，强化政治纪律和政治规矩，增强政治意识、大局意识、核心意识、看齐意识，坚定道路自信、理论自信、制度自信、文化自信，确保绝对忠诚、绝对纯洁、绝对可靠，确保枪杆子永远听党指挥。

regarding national defense and the military.

The people's armed forces must act on the CMC chairperson responsibility system in all respects. We must strengthen political discipline and political rules, heighten our political awareness, develop our ability to have a broader picture, follow the leadership core, and align all activities with the agenda of the central leadership. We must also strengthen our confidence in the path we take, the theory that guides us forward, the political system we choose, and the culture we nurture. In short, we must ensure the purity and reliability of the armed forces, and their absolute loyalty and allegiance to the Party.

政治工作永远是人民军队的生命线

人民军队政治工作，实质上是中国共产党领导和掌握军队的工作，萌芽于大革命时期，创立于建军之初，奠基于古田会议。1929年12月，毛泽东起草的红四军第九次党代表大会决议案，即古田会议决议，第一次系统规定了思想建党、政治建军的基本方针原则，奠定了人民军队政治工作的基础。在长期革命、建设、改革历程中，中国共产党领导的革命的政治工作是革命军队的生命线。实行革命的政治工作，保证了人民军队始终是党的绝对领导下的军队，为人民军队战胜强大敌人和艰难险阻提供了不竭力量，使人民军队始终保持了本色和作风。历史和实践证明，政治工作是人民军队的看家本领，是人民军队的最大特色、最大优势。无论战争形态怎么演变、军队建设内外环境怎么变化、

Political Work as the Lifeblood of the People's Armed Forces

Political work ensures the CPC's leadership over the armed forces. This principle can be traced back to the revolution of the 1920s. It was developed soon after the founding of the Red Army, and was confirmed at the Gutian Meeting. A resolution known as the Gutian Meeting Resolution, drafted by Mao Zedong and adopted at the Ninth Congress of Party Representatives of the Fourth Army of the Red Army, outlined for the first time a systematic framework guiding political work in the armed forces.

Over the long years of revolution, economic and social development and reform, political work under the leadership of the CPC has been the lifeblood of the armed forces. It ensures their absolute loyalty to the Party, provides an inexhaustible source of strength to overcome heavy odds and confront daunting challenges, and ensures that the people's armed forces always adhere to their nature and fine conduct.

It has been proved in history by our practice that political work is what empowers the people's armed forces. It is their most salient characteristic and greatest strength. Whatever changes to the way wars are fought, whatever changes to the domestic and

军队组织形态怎么调整，政治工作永远是人民军队的生命线。

international environment, whatever changes to their organizational structure, political work will always be their lifeblood.

古田全军政治工作会议

2014年10月30日至11月2日，习近平带领全军高级干部在古田这个具有标志性意义的地方，召开全军政治工作会议。会议贯彻整风精神，着力研究解决新的历史条件下党从思想上政治上建设军队的重大问题，弘扬人民军队政治工作的光荣传统和优良作风，动员全军为实现党在新形势下的强军目标而团结奋斗。

习近平在会上发表重要讲话，明确紧紧围绕实现中华民族伟大复兴的中国梦，为实现强军目标提供坚强政治保证的政治工作时代主题，提出把理想信念、党性原则、战斗力标准、政治工作威信4个带根本性的东西在全军牢固立起来，强调着力抓好铸牢军魂工作、高中级干部管理、作风建设和反腐败斗争、战斗精神培育、政治工作创新发展等5个方面。会议形成《关于

The Military Political Work Conference in Gutian

From October 30 to November 2, 2014, a Military Political Work Conference was held in Gutian, a historically significant town in east China's Fujian Province, attended by Xi Jinping and senior military leaders. The conference emphasized the importance of political ethics, and discussed measures the Party should take to raise political awareness in the military in the new era, keep alive the great tradition of political work, and mobilize all military personnel to join the Party's effort to strengthen the military in response to new realities.

Addressing the conference, Xi Jinping highlighted the contemporary relevance of political work, since it provides strong support for the Party's goal of building a strong military as part of the effort to realize the Chinese Dream of national renewal. He emphasized the need to bolster confidence in the Party's ideals, demonstrate commitment to Party principles, improve combat capabilities, and strengthen the authority of military political work. He also outlined measures to cement political loyalty of the military, strengthen the accountability of mid-level and senior officers, improve ethics, combat corruption, promote morale and fighting spirit, and update political

新形势下军队政治工作若干问题的决定》，中共中央转发全党。会议确立了中国共产党在强国强军征程中政治建军的大方略，开拓了中国共产党从思想上政治上建设和掌握军队的新境界，揭开了人民军队以整风精神固本开新的新篇章。

work in a creative way.

A decision on strengthening political work in the military under new conditions was adopted at the conference and distributed Party-wide by the Central Committee. The conference provides a strategic framework for the CPC's political awareness initiatives to boost efforts to build a strong country and a strong military, and opens a new chapter in invigorating and breathing fresh life into the ethical traditions of the people's armed forces.

传承红色基因

红色基因，是中国共产党人的精神内核，是中国军队性质宗旨本色和优良传统的集中体现。

2013年2月，习近平视察兰州军区时提出，要把红色基因一代代传下去。2014年10月，习近平在古田全军政治工作会议上强调，要把理想信念的火种、红色传统的基因一代代传下去。2017年8月1日，习近平在庆祝中国人民解放军建军90周年大会上发表重要讲话，提出人民军队从胜利走向胜利，彰显了中国共产党领导的伟大力量，彰显了理想信念的伟大力量，彰显了改革创新的伟大力量，彰显了战斗精神的伟大力量，彰显了革命纪律的伟大力量，彰显了军民团结的伟大力量，由此对红色基因进行了深刻阐述。

2017年10月，中国共产党第十九次全国代表大会提出，在全军部队开展“传承红色基因、担当强军重任”主题教育。2018年6月，中央军委印发的《传承红色基因实施纲要》明确指出：传承红色基

Traditions of Revolution

The red gene, traditions of revolution, is what informs the convictions of the CPC, and is embedded in the founding ideals and fine tradition of China's armed forces.

While inspecting the Lanzhou Military Zone in February 2013, Xi Jinping urged continued efforts to pass on the red gene. Addressing the Military Political Work Conference in Gutian in October 2014, he repeated the call, emphasizing the importance of boosting confidence in the military's founding ideals and keeping alive its fine tradition.

In his speech to the meeting celebrating the 90th anniversary of the founding of the PLA on August 1, 2017, he further explained why the red gene was important, adding that it ensured victory for the people's armed forces, stood as a testament to the CPC's leadership strengths, instilled confidence in the Party's ideals, inspired reform and innovation, boosted morale and fighting spirit, strengthened discipline, and helped build strong military-civilian relations.

At its 19th National Congress in October 2017, the CPC mandated an education campaign under the theme of "passing on the traditions of revolution and stepping up to the task of making the military strong." In June 2018 the CMC issued implementation guidelines on this topic, reiterating that

因，要着力锻造维护核心、听党指挥的绝对忠诚，坚定社会主义、共产主义的理想信念，强化勇于改革、敢于突破的创新意识，培育一不怕苦、二不怕死的战斗精神，严明高度自觉、令行禁止的革命纪律，巩固爱民为民、军民团结的特有优势。

passing on the red gene was meant to ensure absolute loyalty to the Party and the core leadership of the CPC Central Committee, build up confidence in socialist and communist ideals, cultivate the courage to pursue reform and innovation and to make breakthroughs, develop the service personnel's fighting spirit and tenacity to overcome heavy odds and confront any danger, enforce strict discipline, including self-discipline, and strengthen unity between the military and civilians, including promoting a culture of service to the people.

打造强军文化

强军文化源自中华优秀传统文化，熔铸于中国共产党领导人民创造的革命文化和社会主义先进文化，植根于强军兴军的伟大实践。

2014年10月，习近平在古田全军政治工作会议上强调，要结合各部队传统和任务特点，加强军事文化建设，打造强军文化，培养官兵大无畏的英雄气概和英勇顽强的战斗作风。2014年12月，中共中央转发《关于新形势下军队政治工作若干问题的决定》，明确要求打造具有军队特色、彰显时代精神、支撑打赢制胜的强军文化，塑造中国心、民族魂、强军志。打造强军文化，必须以习近平新时代中国特色社会主义思想为指导，深入贯彻习近平强军思想，大力培育和践行社会主义核心价值观，始终聚焦备战打仗，着力培养有

The Culture That Favors the Development of a Strong Military

The culture that favors the development of a strong military can find its origin in the Chinese tradition. It was born during China's revolution and socialist development under the leadership of the CPC, and is rooted in the contemporary imperative to build a strong military.

Addressing the Military Political Work Conference in Gutian in October 2014, Xi Jinping emphasized the need to build a culture that enables strong defense capabilities and inspires the courage and tenacity to confront daunting challenges, bearing in mind our military tradition and our duties.

The Decision on Strengthening Political Work in the Military Under New Conditions issued by the Central Committee in December 2014 reiterates the importance of building a culture that responds to the specific needs of the military, fits a contemporary context, supports efforts to enhance defense capabilities, and upholds the values of our nation and military. Efforts to build such a culture must be guided by Xi Jinping Thought on Socialism with Chinese Characteristics for a New Era, help cultivate core socialist values, and focus on combat readiness and

灵魂、有本事、有血性、有品德的新时代革命军人，统筹推进文化内容建设、平台建设、力量建设和制度建设，为实现中国梦强军梦提供强大价值引导力、文化凝聚力、精神推动力。

training officers and soldiers of the new era with faith, ability, courage, and integrity. Measures in this connection should include integrated development of necessary platforms, institutional arrangements and resources for creating better cultural products to solicit strength to guide and push the move to realize the Chinese Dream and the dream of building a strong military.

培育战斗精神

人民军队以敢打敢拼闻名于世，在长期革命建设实践中，培育形成了特色鲜明的战斗精神，集中体现为“一不怕苦、二不怕死”。2013年4月，习近平在视察海军驻三亚部队时提出，抓思想政治建设，必须把培育战斗精神、培养战斗作风突出出来，强化官兵当兵打仗、带兵打仗、练兵打仗的思想，探索形成战斗精神培育的长效机制。2014年12月，中共中央转发《关于新形势下军队政治工作若干问题的决定》，强调培育以“一不怕苦、二不怕死”为核心的战斗精神，发挥思想教育引导、训练管理磨砺、重大任务锤炼、战斗文化熏陶、政策制度激励的作用，组织学习部队战史、战例、战将、战斗英雄，弘扬爱国主义和革命英雄主义，提振革命军人精

Cultivation of a Strong Fighting Spirit

Our people's armed forces are known for their ability to fight and win. The undeniable strength of their fighting spirit has been tested over the long years of revolution and economic development. They dare to beat any odds, and dare to confront any danger.

While inspecting the naval forces stationed in Sanya in April 2013, Xi Jinping emphasized the importance of cultivating a strong fighting spirit as an essential element of a political awareness initiative as well as a measure to strengthen the capabilities of service members to fight, to command, and to train, and urged the implementation of long-term mechanisms for developing that spirit.

The Decision on Strengthening Political Work in the Military Under New Conditions outlines a comprehensive framework for developing this spirit through efforts to raise political awareness, tough training, strict discipline, enabling cultural environment, personal involvement in actual operations, and institutional incentives. To this end, training sessions will be organized to examine military history, conduct case studies of wars and conflicts, and read stories of exemplary commanders and war heroes. This will inspire patriotism and heroism, prepare our service members to fight and win wars with the

气神，培育舍身报国战斗信念、敢打必胜战斗血性、团结协作战斗品格、沉稳坚韧战斗心理、英勇顽强战斗作风。

courage to make the ultimate sacrifice for the nation, and to build a strong team spirit, and foster grit, tenacity, and perseverance.

构建完善军人荣誉体系

2017年10月18日，习近平在中国共产党第十九次全国代表大会的报告中提出，推进军人荣誉体系建设，让军人成为全社会尊崇的职业。军人荣誉体系建设，旨在增强军事职业吸引力和军人使命感、荣誉感，以更好凝聚军心、稳定部队、鼓舞士气，主要包括加强退役军人保障工作、完善军人优待政策、健全烈士褒扬机制、加强全民国防教育、完善军队奖励表彰制度、规范军队重要仪式活动、强化军营文化熏陶等内容。

Military Honors System

In his report to the 19th CPC National Congress, Xi Jinping unveiled a plan to develop the military honors system ensuring that service members are held in high regard. Measures to ensure respect for service members are considered necessary to attract more qualified people into military services and develop service personnel's dedication and sense of honor, so as to provide better cohesion, increase retention, and boost morale. Such measures should include, among others, better veteran services, preferential policies for military personnel, tributes to families of those who have made the ultimate sacrifice, efforts to raise public awareness about the importance of national defense, creation of a military awards system, organization of major military ceremonies and events, and nurture of an inspiring military culture.

培养“四有”新时代革命军人

2014年10月，习近平在古田全军政治工作会议上提出，要适应强军目标要求，把握新形势下铸魂育人的特点和规律，着力培养有灵魂、有本事、有血性、有品德的新一代革命军人。有灵魂就是要信念坚定、听党指挥，有本事就是要素质过硬、能打胜仗，有血性就是要英勇顽强、不怕牺牲，有品德就是要情趣高尚、品行端正。这深刻回答了强国强军需要什么样的军人、怎样培养新时代革命军人的重大问题。

Revolutionary Officers and Soldiers of the New Era with Faith, Ability, Courage, and Integrity

Addressing the Military Political Work Conference in Gutian, Xi Jinping called for training officers and soldiers of the new era with faith, ability, courage, and integrity, bearing in mind our goal of building a strong military and personnel development challenges under new conditions. The members of this force are expected to show an unwavering commitment to the Party's cause and obey the Party's orders, be well-trained and able to fight and win tough wars, display the courage to confront any danger, and have moral integrity.

These are the qualities we are trying to reinforce in our service members who will be a pillar in our effort to build a strong country and a strong military.

锻造“四铁”过硬部队

2016年1月，习近平视察陆军部队时，要求锻造具有铁一般信仰、铁一般信念、铁一般纪律、铁一般担当的过硬部队。铁一般信仰，就是坚定对马克思主义的信仰，毫不动摇地坚持党对人民军队的绝对领导的根本原则和制度，在思想上政治上行动上始终与党中央、中央军委保持高度一致，做到在任何时候任何情况下都坚决听从党中央、中央军委指挥；铁一般信念，就是坚定对社会主义和共产主义的信念，坚定对中国特色社会主义的信念，做到信念不动摇、思想不松懈、斗志不衰退、作风不涣散，始终保持坚定的革命意志和旺盛的战斗精神；铁一般纪律，就是厉行法治、严肃军纪，严格遵守政治纪律、组织纪律、廉洁纪律、群众纪律、工作纪律、生活纪律等各项纪律，让铁规生威、铁纪发力，做到令行禁止、步调一致；

Troops with Ironclad Faith, Conviction, Discipline, and Commitment

While inspecting the PLA Army (PLAA) troops in January 2016, Xi Jinping called for building ironclad troops with an unshakeable faith in Marxism, a strong conviction in the socialist and communist cause, strict discipline, and a firm commitment to their duties.

An ironclad faith in Marxism ensures that the military is placed under the absolute leadership of the Party, and that it aligns all its activities, whether ideological, political or operational, with the objectives of the CPC Central Committee and the CMC, and obeys orders from the Party Central Committee and the CMC at all times and under any circumstances.

An ironclad conviction in the socialist and communist cause means unwavering support for socialism with Chinese characteristics and an unwavering determination to do whatever is necessary to pursue the Party's objectives.

An ironclad discipline entails respect for law-based governance and exercise of strict Party and military rules. It also requires promoting political ethics, rooting out corruption, strengthening military-civilian relations, and developing a strong work ethic and personal integrity.

铁一般担当，就是担当起维护国家主权、安全、发展利益的重大责任，牢记使命、奋发进取，做到能打仗、打胜仗，为实现“两个一百年”奋斗目标、实现中华民族伟大复兴的中国梦提供坚强力量保证。

An ironclad commitment to defending national sovereignty, security, and development interests enables the armed forces to be ready and able to fight and win wars, bearing in mind that their mission is to provide reliable support for the realization of the Chinese Dream of national renewal.

坚持全面从严治党、全面从严治军

中国共产党第十八次全国代表大会以来，习近平作出坚持全面从严治党、全面从严治军的重大决策部署，推动管党治党、建军治军从宽松软走向严紧硬。从严治军关键是从严治党，从军队党的建设抓起，以从严治党的实际成效促进从严治军方针的贯彻落实。

人民军队坚决维护习近平总书记党中央的核心、全党的核心地位，坚决维护党中央权威和集中统一领导，贯彻军委主席负责制，落实新时代党的建设总要求，加强党的政治建设，把全面从严要求贯彻到军队建设各方面和全过程。坚持党对人民军队的绝对领导，确保绝对忠诚、绝对纯洁、绝对可靠；坚持以整风精神推进政治整训，着力整顿思想、整顿用人、整顿组织、整顿纪律，重振军队政治纲纪、纯正军队政治生态；坚持以理论武装凝心聚

Strict Governance over the Party and the Military

Since the 18th CPC National Congress, Xi Jinping has made major policy moves to enforce stricter discipline within the Party and the military. The key to building unbreakable discipline within the military lies in stricter discipline within the Party. Stronger and better disciplined Party organizations within the military ensure effective implementation of measures to strengthen discipline across military units.

For its part the military has expressed unequivocal support for General Secretary Xi Jinping's core leadership role within the Central Committee and the Party as a whole, for the Central Committee's authority and centralized and unified leadership, and for the CMC chairperson responsibility system. It is committed to implementing the guidelines for strengthening the Party and its political awareness activities, and enforcing strict discipline across all areas and all steps of its endeavors.

The Party's absolute leadership over the military is to be respected to ensure its absolute loyalty, purity, and reliability. It is critical to keep alive its ethical tradition and promote political ethics, and pursue reform in ideological education, personnel

魂，锻造具有铁一般信仰、铁一般信念、铁一般纪律、铁一般担当的过硬部队；坚持把党组织搞坚强，增强各级组织创造力、凝聚力、战斗力；坚持贯彻军队好干部标准，培养选拔对党忠诚、善谋打仗、敢于担当、实绩突出、清正廉洁的好干部；坚持正风肃纪、反腐惩恶，铲除不正之风和腐败滋生土壤。突出依法治军从严治军，狠抓条令条例和规章制度贯彻落实，下大气力治松、治散、治虚、治软，推动治军方式根本性转变。2018年8月，中央军委党的建设会议召开，强调全面加强新时代军队党的领导和党的建设工作。通过大力推动全面从严治党、全面从严治军，军队政治生态焕然一新，正规化建设取得明显进步，为强军事业提供了坚强政治保证和法治保障。

management, organizational structures, and discipline enforcement. It is also critical to ensure cohesion among military personnel by raising political awareness, and build troops with ironclad faith, conviction, discipline, and commitment. To this end, strengthening the Party organizations is a must, so that they are better able to achieve innovative results and mobilize efforts around the Party's objectives. A sound promotion system is indispensable. Promotion standards should include loyalty to the Party, military expertise, leadership capability, performance records, and moral integrity. Ethical rules must be enforced to fight corruption and other irregularities, and eradicate any cells of corruption. Law-based governance will be pursued with a focus on effective implementation of rules and regulations. Strong measures will be taken to correct misconducts such as negligence or dereliction of duty. A fundamental change in military governance is expected.

The CMC convened a conference in August 2018, emphasizing the need to strengthen the Party and its leadership role in the military in the new era. An overall push to strengthen discipline within the Party and the military ensures the creation of a new ecosystem in the military that helps the modernization process and provides firm political and legal assurance for the Party to build a strong military.

军队正风肃纪反腐

腐败动摇的是军心，锈蚀的是战斗力，与人民军队性质宗旨格格不入，与军队职能使命水火不容。军队是拿枪杆子的，绝不允许有腐败分子藏身之地。

中国共产党第十八次全国代表大会以来，习近平领导人民军队坚定不移推进正风肃纪反腐。严明政治纪律政治规矩，严肃查处郭伯雄、徐才厚、房峰辉、张阳等严重违纪违法案件。严格依纪依法惩治腐败，开展重大工程建设、装备物资采购等行业领域专项整治，扭住重要节点持续开展作风督查，深入纠“四风”正风气。建立基层风气监察联系点制度，把正风肃纪反腐压力传导到基层，着力纠治官兵身边“微腐败”和不正之风。全面推开巡视巡察工作，深化政治巡视，强化政治监督，

Enforcement of Ethical Standards and Anti-Corruption Measures

Corruption saps morale and erodes military capability. It runs counter to the military's objectives, and harms its functions. As a fighting force, the military should not be a place where corruption thrives.

Since the 18th CPC National Congress, a series of anti-corruption measures have been rolled out under the leadership of Xi Jinping in the military, resulting in the removal of some high-ranking officers found to have committed serious violations, including Guo Boxiong, Xu Caihou, Fang Fenghui, and Zhang Yang.

In addition to measures to punish corruption in accordance with applicable laws and regulations, efforts are also underway to reform processes by which major construction projects and procurement plans are implemented with a focus on scrutiny and accountability to curtail and combat any irregularities. A network of focal points is now in place to monitor the enforcement of ethical standards at primary-level units and help stamp out any "micro corruption" and misconducts among service members.

Other moves include more inspections and strengthened oversight, especially inspections, and re-inspections over all

完成对军委机关部门、大单位巡视和回访巡视全覆盖，紧跟形势任务要求开展专项巡视。着力推进审计全覆盖，加大重点领域、重大项目、重要资金审计力度，严格领导干部经济责任审计，积极推行经费绩效审计、全程跟踪审计、军地联合审计。反腐败斗争取得压倒性胜利，风清气正的良好政治生态基本形成。

CMC functional organs, theater commands, services, military academies and universities, and the People's Armed Police Force (PAP), and ad hoc inspections as part of special enforcement campaigns.

Auditing will be conducted in all areas, especially with regard to major projects and where large sums of money are involved. Ranking officers will be subject to rigorous financial audits. Auditing will cover budget performance. In some cases, it can cover entire budgeting cycles or project life cycles. Audits can be performed jointly by military and civilian auditors. The anti-corruption campaign has secured an overwhelming victory, and a healthy political ethics ecosystem has emerged.

军政军民团结

军政军民团结是中国军队在长期革命建设发展实践中形成的优良传统和特有优势，本质和核心是始终保持中国共产党绝对领导下的人民军队同人民群众的血肉联系。毛泽东曾作出“军民团结如一人，试看天下谁能敌”的著名论断。2013年3月，习近平在十二届全国人大一次会议解放军代表团全体会议上指出，军政军民团结是实现富国与强军相统一的重要政治保障。

军政军民团结包括相辅相成的两个方面：一是军队践行全心全意为人民服务的宗旨，遵守秋毫无犯的群众纪律，拥护政府，爱护人民；二是地方政府和人民群众拥护军队，爱护军人，优待军属。解放战争的淮海战役中，支援部队作战的群众达540多万，就是军民团结如一人的生动

Strong Military-Civil Bond

Strong military-civil bond is a time-honored tradition and the military's unique strength developed over the long years of revolution and development. It entails the persistent connection between the CPC-led military and the people. Mao Zedong once said, "When the military and the people are united as one, they are unrivaled." Addressing the plenary meeting of the PLA delegates to the first session of the 12th NPC on March 11, 2013, Xi Jinping pointed out that intensified military-civil relations provided indispensable support for efforts to build a strong country and a strong military.

The military-civil bond unfolds in two mutually reinforcing aspects. First, the military fulfils its duties to protect and serve – and never harm – the people's interests, and cooperates with local governments. Second, local governments and the public support and respect the military and give preferential treatment to families of service members. A notable example of such relationship is the participation of 5.4 million civilians in supporting the PLA's Huaihai Campaign (1948-1949) during the War of Liberation. Our military always stands with our people. Together, we have responded to natural disasters, such as the devastating floods

体现。人民军队始终和人民同呼吸、共命运、心连心，“98”抗洪、四川汶川抗震救灾、西部大开发、脱贫攻坚战、抗击新冠肺炎疫情等，都是生动写照。历史证明，坚如磐石的军政军民关系，是战胜一切艰难险阻、不断从胜利走向胜利的重要法宝。

of 1998 and the Wenchuan earthquake of 2008. Together, we have fought the Covid-19 pandemic in 2020. Together, we have forged ahead with the development program for western regions and anti-poverty campaigns.

History shows that with rock-solid military-civil relations there will be no insurmountable hurdles, and nothing will stop us going from victory to victory.

参加抢险救灾

参加国家建设事业、保卫人民和平劳动，是宪法赋予中国武装力量的使命任务。依据《军队参加抢险救灾条例》，中国武装力量主要担负解救、转移或者疏散受困人员，保护重要目标安全，抢救、运送重要物资，参加道路（桥梁、隧道）抢修、海上搜救、核生化救援、疫情控制、医疗救护等专业抢险，排除或者控制其他危重险情、灾情，必要时可以协助地方人民政府开展灾后重建工作等任务。

2012年以来，截至2019年7月，解放军和武警部队共出动95万人次，组织民兵141万人次，动用车辆及工程机械19万台次、船艇2.6万艘次、飞机（直升机）820架次参加抢险救灾。先后参加云南鲁甸地震救灾、长江中下游暴雨洪涝灾害抗洪抢

Emergency Rescue and Disaster Relief

Participating in national development and protecting the people's rights to work in peace are the responsibilities of China's armed forces mandated by the Constitution.

The duties the military may be called on to perform, as provided for in the Regulations on Participation in Emergency Rescue and Disaster Relief by China's Armed Forces, include, among others, rescuing, transferring and evacuating trapped populations; ensuring the security of important targets; salvaging and transporting important materials; conducting specialized operations such as restoration of transportation facilities including roads, bridges and tunnels, maritime search and rescue, NBC rescue, epidemic control and medical relief; avoiding or controlling other major threats and disasters; and supporting civil authorities in post-disaster reconstruction on request.

From 2012 to July 2019, the PLA and the PAP deployed 950,000 soldiers, 1.41 million militia, 190,000 vehicles and items of equipment, and sortied 26,000 vessels and 820 aircraft in emergency response and disaster relief. Among major operations, the military responded to the Ludian earthquake, the floods along the middle and lower reaches of the Yangtze River, and the formation of

险、雅鲁藏布江堰塞湖排险等救灾救援行动，协助地方政府解救、转移安置群众500余万人，巡诊救治病员21万余人次，抢运物资36万余吨，加固堤坝3600余千米。2017年，驻澳门部队出动兵力2631人次，车辆160余台次，协助特别行政区政府开展强台风“天鸽”灾后救援。

a landslide dam that blocked the Yarlung Zangbo River. During these operations, the military assisted local governments in the evacuation of 5 million people, provided medical care for 210,000 people, transported 360,000 tons of supplies, and reinforced dams totaling 3,600 kilometers in length. In 2017, 2,631 troops and 160 vehicles of the PLA Macao Garrison participated in the disaster relief operations launched by the Macao Special Administrative Region government in the aftermath of Super Typhoon Hato.

战斗力标准

能打仗、打胜仗是党和人民对军队的根本要求，是军队使命职责之所在、军队存在的根本价值之所在。习近平强调，军队是要打仗的，要牢固树立战斗力这个唯一的根本的标准。中国军队坚持把战斗力标准贯彻到全军各项建设和工作之中，坚持把提高战斗力作为全军各项建设的出发点和落脚点，坚持用是否有利于提高战斗力来衡量和检验各项工作，使各项建设和工作向实现建设信息化军队、打赢信息化战争的战略目标聚焦，向实施一体化联合作战的要求聚焦，向形成基于网络信息体系的联合作战能力、全域作战能力聚焦。

Combat Effectiveness as the Criterion

The Party and the people want our military to be able to fight and win wars, and this is the fundamental requirement for the military. Possession of this ability enables the military to fulfill its duties.

As Xi Jinping pointed out, the military is built to fight, and combat effectiveness is the sole and fundamental criterion of all military endeavors. Efforts to build combat capabilities should therefore be placed at the heart of all of the military's activities, viewed as the starting point as well as the end objective, and used as a yardstick for evaluation. It is essential in this regard to adapt the Chinese military to the information age, and align all activities with the goal of building a strong military with joint operations capabilities based on network-enabled information systems, able to operate in multiple domains and win informationized wars.

人民战争

人民战争是指反抗外来侵略或维护国家统一，武装和依靠广大人民群众，反映人民群众自身利益和意志的战争。“兵民是胜利之本”。以毛泽东为代表的中国共产党人，在长期的革命战争和军事实践中，全面发展马克思主义的人民战争理论，形成了具有中国特色的人民战争思想。信息化战争具有平战一体、前后方一体、军民一体的显著特点，实行人民战争具有广阔舞台。习近平指出，不论形势如何发展，人民战争这个法宝永远不能丢，要把握新的时代条件下人民战争的新特点新要求，创新内容和方式方法，充分发挥人民战争的整体威力。

People's War

People's war refers to confronting foreign aggression or safeguarding national unity by arming and relying on the people. It reflects the people's resolve to protect their own interests.

The army and the people are the foundation of victory, and the concept that the people's participation in a war ensures victory was developed by Chinese Communists represented by Mao Zedong during the long years of revolutionary wars. It enriches Marxist theory about people's war, and is a doctrine unique to China. Informationized wars are characterized by the blurred lines between peacetime and wartime, war zone and rear area, and combatants and civilians, providing a wide stage for people's war.

As Xi Jinping reaffirmed, we should never ditch our magic weapon that is people's war, however the environment we find ourselves in changes. Instead we should tap its full potential in the new era by responding to new dynamics and new imperatives, and developing new techniques and tools and incorporating them in our people's war strategy in an innovative manner.

积极防御战略思想

积极防御战略思想是中国共产党军事战略思想的基本点，是中国指导军事斗争和军事力量运用的根本方针。在长期革命战争实践中，人民军队形成了一整套积极防御战略思想，坚持战略上防御与战役战斗上进攻的统一，坚持防御、自卫、后发制人的原则，坚持“人不犯我、我不犯人，人若犯我、我必犯人”。中国是社会主义国家，奉行和平外交政策，坚持走和平发展道路，从根本上决定了在战略上始终是积极防御。坚持积极防御战略思想，必须从时代条件出发，丰富和完善积极防御战略思想的内涵，更加有效地塑造态势、管控危机、遏制战争、打赢战争。

A Strategic Concept of Active Defense

The concept of active defense underpins the CPC's military strategy and guides China's decision-making in relation to the use of military force.

It was developed by the people's military in the long years of revolutionary wars. It calls for a balance between a strategic defensive posture and offensives in battles and campaigns, and focuses on self-defense, that is, the use of military force only for defensive purposes and only when we are attacked. In other words, "we will not attack unless we are attacked; if we are attacked, we will certainly counterattack."

As a socialist country, China promotes peace in international relations and pursues peaceful development, and it is natural that our defense policy is defensive in nature. The concept of active defense should be enriched by taking into account contemporary imperatives, so that we can deter wars, respond to any crises that may emerge, and win wars when they do occur.

战争与和平的辩证法

2013年3月11日，习近平在十二届全国人大一次会议解放军代表团全体会议上指出，能战方能止战，准备打才可能不必打，越不能打越可能挨打，这就是战争与和平的辩证法。当今世界，维护和平的力量在上升，制约战争的因素在增多，但是世界依然面临现实和潜在的战争威胁，和平必须以强大实力为后盾，能打赢才能有力遏制战争。中国人民珍爱和平，坚定不移走和平发展道路，中国军队始终是维护世界和平的坚定力量。中国渴望和平，但决不会因此而放弃我们的正当权益，决不会拿国家的核心利益做交易。中国决不干称王称霸的事，决不会搞侵略扩张，但如果有人要把战争强加到我们头上，我们必须能决战决胜。

Dialectics of War and Peace

Addressing the plenary meeting of the PLA delegates to the first session of the 12th NPC on March 11, 2013, Xi Jinping explained the dialectic of war and peace, which tells us that only those who can fight can stop war, and only when we are prepared for war can we prevent war from happening, and that war will be upon us if we are weak.

Today, while the forces that promote peace and prevent war are on the rise, the world still faces actual and potential threats of war. Peace can only be ensured by strength. Only the ability to win wars can deter wars.

The Chinese people love peace, and will never waver in their pursuit of peaceful development. China's armed forces are always a pillar of world peace. China craves peace, but our legitimate rights and core national interests are non-negotiable. While China will never seek hegemony or expansion, or engage in aggression, we will have to fight back and win if a war is imposed on us.

实战化军事训练

军事训练是提高实战能力的重要途径和抓手，是最直接的军事斗争准备。习近平多次强调，坚持从难从严训练部队，切实提高军事训练实战化水平；贯彻战训一致原则，坚持仗怎么打兵就怎么练，打仗需要什么就苦练什么，部队最缺什么就专攻精练什么。2014年3月中央军委印发《关于提高军事训练实战化水平的意见》，2016年11月中央军委印发《加强实战化军事训练暂行规定》，明确了当前和今后一个时期提高军事训练实战化水平的指导思想、总体思路、主要任务和措施要求。

实战化军事训练，是遵循制胜机理和练兵规律，在近似实战的环境和条件下进行训练。本质内涵是按实战要求训练，按训练去实战，使训练与实战达到一体化。在训练实践中，坚持聚焦实战、对接实战，坚持实战实训、联战联训，把从难从严按纲施训作为提升实战化军事训练水平的重要抓手，紧贴作战任务、作战对手、

Realistic Military Training

Military training is key to enhancing combat capabilities and combat readiness. As Xi Jinping has repeatedly emphasized, rigorous training is indispensable, and it is essential to improve realistic training, aligned with actual war scenarios, to ensure the relevance of training, and identify and focus on what we need most in hostile situations.

The CMC issued the Guidelines for Improving Military Training Under Real Combat Conditions in March 2014 and the Provisionary Rules on Strengthening Realistic Military Training in November 2016, outlining guiding principles, underlying considerations, major tasks and requirements for improving current and future training for real war scenarios.

Training for real combat is how military training should be done to ensure its effectiveness. It means that training should be conducted under conditions similar to real combat situations to meet real combat needs, so that training routines can be executed in actual operations to adapt the former to fit the latter. Specifically, the focus will be on the use of realistic combat scenarios in training, including joint operations scenarios. Units of the military will carry out rigorous, hyper-realistic training in

作战环境，加强对抗性检验性训练，加强针对性适应性训练，大力开展战法创新，提高备战打仗能力。

accordance with tailored training outlines that corresponds to their duties and mimics actual combat environments to test and verify the effectiveness of training. It is also important to encourage innovation in combat solutions.

纠治和平积弊

一支军队在长期相对和平的环境中，容易形成偏离打仗中心的思想、行为和状态，积因成弊，具有一定普遍性和顽固性。习近平要求全军大力纠治和平积弊。为此，中国军队以整风精神开展“和平积弊大起底大扫除”活动，扭住能打仗、打胜仗这个关键，查找和纠治备战打仗突出矛盾问题，坚决克服背离实战的思想和行为，官兵当兵打仗、带兵打仗、练兵打仗思想不断强化，在备战打仗上有很大的加强。

Efforts to Uproot Peacetime Ills

A long period of relative peace can easily leave a military moored in accumulated inertia, diminishing its combat readiness and rendering it ill-prepared for action, both mentally and operationally.

Xi Jinping has urged the military to avoid this inertia. In response to his call, a vigorous campaign has been launched to bring about fundamental change in the way the military readies itself to take on and neutralize actual threats. It focuses on identifying and addressing major issues and vulnerabilities that contribute to the peacetime ills and chip away at combat readiness. As a result, service members focus more on their duties to fight, to command and to train, bringing the military to a significantly higher level of preparedness.

反恐维稳

中国《宪法》《国防法》《反恐怖主义法》等明确赋予中国武装力量依法防范和处置恐怖活动的职责，赋予中国人民武装警察部队担负国家安全保卫任务、维护社会秩序的职责，赋予中国人民解放军依法协助维护社会秩序的职责。近年来，中国武装力量积极构建反恐怖专业力量体系，成立了“猎鹰”、“雪豹”突击队等专业应急力量，不断提升应急处置能力，依法成功参与处置一系列恐怖袭击事件，稳妥应对一系列公共卫生和社会安全等突发事件，确保了国家安全、公共安全、环境安全和社会安全。

恐怖主义是全人类的公敌，没有任何国家能够独自应对，也没有任何国家可以独善其身。中国反对一切形式的恐怖主义。中国武装力量遵守《联合国宪章》和国际法准则，支持联合国安理会通过的一系列反恐决议，深化与国际和周边地区有

Fighting Terrorism and Maintaining Social Stability

According to China's Constitution, National Defense Law and Anti-terrorism Law, the Chinese armed forces are mandated to prevent and neutralize terrorist activities. The PAP is also mandated to protect national security and the social order, and the PLA is authorized to assist law enforcement when necessary.

In recent years, the PLA and the PAP have stepped up efforts to develop specialized counter-terrorism units, including the establishment of special rapid response teams, such as the Falcon Commando and the Snow Leopard Commando. These efforts have resulted in a steady improvement in emergency response capability, and ensured success in a series of counter-terrorism attacks, public health challenges and social emergencies. They have successfully performed their duties to protect national security, public security, environmental security, and social stability.

Terrorism is a scourge that ravages the world. No country is able to fight it alone, and no country is immune from terrorist threats. China stands firm in the fight against terrorism in all its forms and expressions.

In compliance with the United Nations

关国家在反恐、执法方面的交流合作，积极参与上合组织、东盟、四国机制等区域组织框架内的双（多）边反恐联演联训，共同提升联合防范和应对恐怖主义威胁的能力，有效维护了国际和地区和平稳定。当今世界恐怖主义愈演愈烈，中国政府和武装力量愿同各方保持积极沟通，持续促进反恐合作，联手应对风险挑战，确保世界和地区的和平与发展。

Charter and UN Security Council resolutions on terrorism, China's armed forces have increased cooperation on counter-terrorism and law-enforcement with neighboring countries and other countries, and actively participated in joint counter-terrorism exercises within bilateral and multilateral frameworks, such as the Shanghai Cooperation Organization (SCO), the ASEAN, and the counter-terrorism quadrilateral cooperation and coordination mechanism by the militaries of Afghanistan, China, Pakistan and Tajikistan (QCCM), to strengthen joint measures to prevent and fight terrorism and protect international and regional peace and stability.

Facing the spread of global terrorism, the Chinese government and armed forces stand ready to increase exchanges and cooperation with other countries to counter terrorist threats and ensure global and regional peace and development.

建设联合、精干、高效的后勤

2016年11月，习近平在中央军委后勤工作会议上强调，着力建设一切为了打仗的后勤，建设联合、精干、高效的后勤。中国军队贯彻落实这一要求，重塑后勤体系，着眼合成化、模块化、体系化、战斗化，推进保障要素合起来、保障模式联起来、保障方式动起来，加快后勤融入联合作战体系步伐。

2016年9月13日，中央军委联勤保障部队成立。其后逐步建立起以联勤保障部队为主干、军种为补充，统分结合、通专两线的保障体制，构建了以战略战役力量为主干、队属力量为补充、社会保障为依托，联合、精干、高效的后勤力量体系，初步形成快速响应、全维参战、精确保障能力，走开精兵保障、精锐制胜之路。

Joint, Capable, and Efficient Logistic Support

Addressing a CMC meeting on logistic support in November 2016, Xi Jinping emphasized the need to build joint, capable and efficient logistic support capabilities ready for war.

Measures in this regard are being implemented to build a combined logistics system that integrates related capabilities in a systematic manner, offers modular solutions, supports readiness for war, and ensures coordination and incorporation of logistics services into joint operations systems.

On September 13, 2016, the CMC established a joint logistic support force. A support mechanism was put in place to combine centralized and decentralized support, as well as general and special-purpose supplies, with the Joint Logistic Support Force (PLAJLSF) as the backbone and service logistics units as supplements. Efforts were also made to build a joint, capable and efficient logistics force structure with the strategic and campaign level logistics units as the main force, branch-affiliated units as the support, and civil resources as supplements. Preliminary results have shown in developing a targeted, streamlined and combat-oriented logistic capability able to respond rapidly.

军队保障社会化

1998年中央军委提出军队后勤保障特别是生活保障必须社会化，1999年试点，2000年在全军推行。中国共产党第十八次全国代表大会以来，中国军队保障社会化范围不断拓展，由后勤领域逐步拓展延伸到军事、政治、装备等领域，由生活保障社会化、后勤保障社会化到军队保障社会化，通过市场机制或采取纳入社会化公共服务体系的形式，在生活保障、通用物资储备、基础设施建设、公务用车、非公务电话通信保障、人才培养、军队文化事业、军人子女教育、军事科研、装备生产和维修保障等方面，初步打破了军队自成体系的保障方式，走开了依托社会保障的路子，取得了明显的军事、经济和社会效益。

The Military's Use of Civilian Service Providers

A plan to outsource part of military logistics services, especially the provision of daily supplies, was unveiled by the CMC in 1998; a pilot program was rolled out in 1999; and the full implementation of the plan started in 2000.

Since the 18th CPC National Congress, the use of civilian providers has been gradually expanded to include other noncombat functions and areas such as military, political, and armament development. The expanded use of civilian providers relies on market mechanisms or existing public services. Services provided by civilian sectors include daily necessities, general supplies, infrastructure projects, transportation services, telephone services for non-official use, talent development, cultural activities, education of military children, defense-related research, and development, and armament production and maintenance, among others. A self-contained supply system has gradually given way to a network that relies on civilian providers, significantly improving efficiency and cost-effectiveness.

军队全面停止有偿服务

2015年11月，中央军委召开改革工作会议，决定军队全面停止开展对外有偿服务。2016年2月中央军委印发《关于军队和武警部队全面停止有偿服务活动的通知》，2018年5月中共中央办公厅、国务院办公厅、中央军委办公厅印发《关于深入推进军队全面停止有偿服务工作的指导意见》，确定到2018年年底前，全面停止解放军和武警部队各级机关、部队及其所属事业单位开展的一切以营利为目的、单纯为社会提供服务的项目。截至2018年6月，军队各级机关、部队及其所属事业单位从事的房地产租赁、农副业生产、招接待等15个行业的有偿服务活动基本停止，超过10万个有偿服务项目按期停止，军队不从事经营活动的目标基本实现。

Discontinuing the Military's Income-Generating Services

At a meeting on reform in November 2015 the CMC decided to discontinue all income-generating services in the military. In February 2016 the CMC issued an official circular banning all income-generating activities within the military and the PAP. In May 2018 the General Office of the Central Committee, the General Office of the State Council, and the General Office of the CMC issued the guidelines for discontinuing income-generating activities in the military, mandating a complete end to all public-oriented, for-profit activities within the PLA and the PAP at all levels and their affiliated institutions. As of June 2018, such activities across 15 industries, including real estate leasing, agricultural production, and hospitality, had been discontinued. More than 100,000 income-generating service entities were closed before specified deadlines. The goal of separating the military from business has basically been achieved.

勤俭建军

中国军队始终坚持贯彻勤俭建军方针，发扬艰苦奋斗精神，坚持勤俭办一切事业，按照节约每一个铜板的精神花好每一分钱，大力推进节能降耗、资源节约工作，厉行节约、反对浪费，提高部队建设精准度和效费比。与世界主要国家相比，中国国防费无论是占国内生产总值和国家财政支出的比重，还是国民人均和军人人均数额，都处于较低水平，需要突出加强军费管理，科学确定投向投量，最大限度地提高经费保障效益，确保财力向战斗力有效转化。

The Virtue of Practicing Economy in Building a Strong Military

China's military always practices economy and never tolerates wasteful conduct. Everything should be done in a way that ensures that no money is wasted and that every cent counts. Measures are in place to conserve energy and other resources, reduce waste, and improve efficiency and cost-effectiveness.

Compared with other major countries, China's defense spending is low, whether as a share of GDP or total government spending, or whether in terms of general per capita spending or spending per service member. Rigorous military budget management is essential to ensuring rational resource allocation and making the most of the available resources.

军事采购国际招标

军事采购国际招标是军队为满足建设发展需要，由军队采购机构或者委托国际招标代理机构，按照规定的程序和组织方法，在国际范围内吸引潜在供应商参与竞争，从中择优选定供应商的采购方式。组织军事采购国际招标，既是适应中国加入WTO政府采购协定（GPA）的必然要求，也是提升军事采购保障效益的有效途径，能够有效促进军事采购公平竞争，丰富军事采购保障资源。自1998年以来，中国军事采购国际招标发展迅速，组织程序和手段机制不断成熟完善，国际招标的范围和规模不断扩大，越来越多的跨国公司积极参与中国军事采购国际招标活动。

International Defense Tenders

International defense tenders are necessary to meet the military's needs. Tenders are conducted by military procurement offices or through international agents according to established procedures and rules, to invite potential international suppliers to bid and to award contracts to the most competitive bidders.

International tendering is required under the World Trade Organization's Government Procurement Agreement to which China is a party. It also helps build a cost-effective military procurement system. Fair competition better ensures efficient acquisition of necessary material and services. Since 1998, international tenders have been increasing in defense-related procurement. Tender procedures and mechanisms have steadily improved. The expanding use of global tenders has attracted an increasing number of multinational corporations to bid for China's defense contracts.

构建现代化武器装备体系

武器装备是军队现代化的重要标志。随着信息技术快速发展，信息化战争成为现代战争的主要形态，体系对抗的特征更加明显。中国军队武器装备贯彻体系建设思想，完善优化武器装备体系结构，统筹推进各军兵种武器装备发展，统筹主战装备、信息系统、保障装备发展，全面提升标准化、系列化、通用化水平。加大淘汰老旧装备力度，逐步形成以高新技术装备为骨干的武器装备体系。

Modern Weaponry Systems

Defense modernization is characterized by, among other things, modern weaponry systems. With the rapid development of information technology, modern warfare manifests itself in informationized wars and increasingly relies on the strength of synchronized operational systems.

It is therefore essential to develop a systematic framework for defense modernization. China's armed forces are optimizing the composition of weaponry and equipment, coordinating efforts of all branches in this regard, promoting balanced development of main battle armament, information systems, and support equipment, and comprehensively update standardization, serial development, and interoperability. Obsolete equipment will be replaced by new high-tech hardware.

网络信息体系

网络信息体系是以网络中心、信息主导、体系支撑为主要特征的复杂巨系统，是信息化作战体系的基本形态，是打赢信息化战争的基础支撑。2017年10月18日，习近平在中国共产党第十九次全国代表大会的报告中提出，提高基于网络信息体系的联合作战能力、全域作战能力。网络信息体系建设，面向联合作战要求，实现要素基于网络互联，信息基于网络共享，功能基于网络融合，行动基于网络协同，牵引重塑指挥体系、力量体系、装备体系和保障体系，大力提升威慑和实战能力，为建设信息化军队、打赢信息化战争提供强有力支撑。

A Network-Enabled Information System

A network-enabled information system is a complex system based on internet technologies and information management, which is expected to help deliver the strength of synchronized operational systems. They are essential to winning informationized warfare.

In his report to the 19th CPC National Congress, Xi Jinping called for improving the military's joint operations capabilities and its ability to operate in different domains by strengthening network-enabled information systems. Efforts to strengthen network-enabled information systems should be geared toward joint operations. They should enable connected operational elements, shared information, integrated functions and coordinated actions, and reconfigure command systems, force structure, armaments, and logistics services. These efforts help strengthen the capabilities to deter, to fight and to prevail in informationized wars.

坚持自主创新的战略基点

2017年8月1日，习近平在庆祝中国人民解放军建军90周年大会上发表重要讲话，强调要全面实施科技兴军战略，坚持自主创新的战略基点。坚持自主创新的战略基点，是在国家创新驱动发展战略指导下，发扬自力更生、自强不息、自我革新的意志和精神，坚持创新这个发展基础，努力建立和完善拥有自主知识产权的核心技术和武器装备体系，不断提高科技创新对人民军队建设和战斗力发展的贡献率。中国军队加快实施科技兴军战略，巩固和加强优势领域，加大新兴领域创新力度，一些战略性、前沿性技术自主创新取得重要进展，成功研制天河二号超级计算机等一批高技术成果。

Innovation as a Strategic Tool

In his speech to the meeting celebrating the 90th anniversary of the founding of the PLA on August 1, 2017, Xi Jinping emphasized the strategic importance of scientific and technological innovation in building a strong military.

Guided by a national strategy for innovation-driven development, a strategic focus on innovation calls for self-reliance, perseverance, and willpower to reinvent ourselves in our push to develop proprietary core technologies and new weaponry systems. Science and technology will contribute more to a stronger military with greater capability.

An innovation strategy is being implemented across the military to build up and leverage existing strengths, and promote innovation in new areas, especially strategically important areas, such as the development and application of frontier technologies. Significant progress has been made in this regard, with an impressive array of research results, such as the rollout of the Tianhe-2 supercomputer.

航母建设发展

航母是以舰载机为主要武器，并作为海上活动基地的大型水面战斗舰艇，是现代海军的重要组成部分。中国海岸线漫长，管辖海域广阔，海洋权益丰富多样，需要建设一支能够保卫国家海上方向安全、维护领海主权和海洋权益的武装力量。

中国已完成对一艘废旧航母平台的改造，并交付海军部队，命名为“辽宁舰”，于2012年9月25日入列服役。中国有关部门在综合考虑各方面因素后，展开第二艘航母的自主研制、设计建造和试验试航工作，第二艘航母于2017年4月26日下水，于2019年12月17日交接入列，命名为“山东舰”。

中国始终坚持走和平发展道路，坚定奉行防御性的国防政策、积极防御的军事战略。中国建设发展航母，是为了维护国家安全，也有利于维护世界和平稳定。中国的国防政策和军事战略决不会因为发展先进武器而改变。

Development of Aircraft Carriers

Aircraft carriers are large surface warships that derive their main capabilities from warplanes on board. They are an important component of a modern navy.

China has a long coastline, an extensive stretch of territorial waters and substantial maritime interests. It is therefore necessary to build a naval force that is able to safeguard China's maritime security, sovereignty over its territorial waters, and maritime interests.

An old carrier hull was refurbished and refitted, and the new carrier, named the *Liaoning,* was commissioned into the PLA Navy (PLAN) on September 25, 2012. Development of a home-designed aircraft carrier proceeded afterward, taking into account relevant factors and lessons learned. The second carrier, the *Shandong,* was launched on April 26, 2017, and was commissioned on December 17, 2019.

China pursues peaceful development. Its defense policy is defensive in nature, underpinned by a military strategy of active defense. Development of aircraft carriers is intended to safeguard national security and contribute to the maintenance of world peace and stability. China's defense policy will not change with the development of advanced weaponry systems.

“东风”系列导弹

“东风”系列导弹是中国火箭军装备使用的导弹武器系统的代称，对外代字为“DF”。中华人民共和国成立之初，为应对外部安全威胁、保卫国家主权和领土完整，决策发展以导弹、原子弹为代表的尖端技术，提高新生人民民主政权的自主防卫能力。中国自20世纪50年代末启动地地战略导弹研制。1960年11月，中国首发地地战略导弹飞行试验成功，标志着已初步具备这类导弹研发能力。1964年，国家和军队有关部门正式对“东风”系列导弹命名进行确认。目前，中国自行研制的“东风”系列导弹，实现了核常兼备、陆海兼备、射程衔接、固液并存和通用化、集成化、信息化。

The DF Missile Family

The Dongfeng (DF) missiles are a series of missiles of different ranges operated by the PLA Rocket Force (PLARF). The missile program was launched in the early days of the People's Republic, together with a program to develop nuclear and other advanced weapons in order to strengthen the ability of the newly established people's government to counter external security threats and defend national sovereignty and territorial integrity.

Development of strategic surface-to-surface missiles started in the late 1950s. The first successful strategic missile test was conducted in November 1960, marking a new milestone in China's development of this type of missile. A naming scheme for missiles was rolled out in 1964, with a prefix "Dongfeng" or DF. Currently, the DF family comprises land-based and sea-based missiles of different ranges, with nuclear and conventional warheads, and with solid and liquid propulsion. The missile program also focuses on interoperability, integration and use of information technology.

深化国防和军队改革

着眼坚持和发展中国特色社会主义、实现中华民族伟大复兴的中国梦，习近平提议把深化国防和军队改革作为全面深化改革的重要组成部分，写入中国共产党十八届三中全会《决定》，上升为党的意志和国家行为。2015年11月24日，习近平在中央军委改革工作会议上对深化国防和军队改革作出全面部署，明确要求着力解决制约国防和军队建设的体制性障碍、结构性矛盾、政策性问题，推进军队组织形态现代化，努力构建能够打赢信息化战争、有效履行使命任务的中国特色现代军事力量体系，完善中国特色社会主义军事制度，为实现“两个一百年”奋斗目标、实现中华民族伟大复兴的中国梦提供坚强力量保证。

在习近平亲自领导、决策和推动下，深化国防和军队改革大刀阔斧、大开大合、大破大立，开启了人民军队整体性、革命性重塑的伟大变革，率先展开领导指

Further Reform in Defense and Military

As suggested by Xi Jinping, the need for further reform in defense and military as part of an expanded in-depth national reform program was incorporated in the Decision of the Third Plenary Session of the 18th CPC Central Committee. The move highlighted the importance of this reform to the development of socialism with Chinese characteristics and the realization of the Chinese Dream of national renewal, thus requiring close attention and substantive involvement by the Party and the state.

Addressing a CMC meeting on reform on November 24, 2015, Xi Jinping unveiled a reform plan to remove institutional barriers, solve structural and policy-related problems, modernize organizational structure, update the military force structure and military system with Chinese features, and create a strong military able to win informationized wars and effectively fulfill its missions. Strong armed forces provide indispensable support for achieving the Two Centenary Goals and realizing the Chinese Dream of national renewal.

With Xi Jinping's personal involvement in guidance and decision-making, defense and military reform has been powering ahead. It is an all-encompassing process, involving

挥体制改革，压茬推进军队规模结构和力量编成改革，着力深化军事政策制度改革。人民军队体制、结构、格局、面貌焕然一新，维护国家主权、安全、发展利益的能力显著增强。

fundamental overhauls of the leadership and command system, and changes to the size, structure, and force composition. Military policies and institutions have also been subject to revision.

These changes have injected fresh life into the military and significantly improved its ability to protect national sovereignty, security, and development interests.

领导指挥体制改革

领导指挥体制改革是适应现代军队专业化分工和信息时代能打仗、打胜仗的要求，提高军队作战效能和建设效益的重大举措。按照“军委管总、战区主战、军种主建”原则，强化军委集中统一领导和战略指挥、战略管理功能，打破长期实行的总部体制、大军区体制、大陆军体制，构建新的军队领导管理和作战指挥体制。

调整组建新的军委机关部门，由过去的四总部调整为军委机关15个职能部门。完善军兵种领导管理体制，成立陆军领导机构，成立战略支援部队，第二炮兵更名为火箭军，成立联勤保障部队，构建起“中央军委—军种—部队”的领导管理体系。

Reform of the Leadership and Command System

The reform of the leadership and command system is a significant measure in response to the call for a modern and specialized military capable of fighting and winning wars in the information age. The goal is to improve the operational effectiveness and development efficiency of the military. Adhering to the general principle of "the CMC exercising overall leadership, the theater commands (TCs) responsible for military operations, and the services focusing on developing capabilities," the PLA upholds the CMC's centralized and unified leadership and its functions of strategic command and management. The PLA has dismantled the long-established systems of general departments, military area commands (MACs) and the force composition with a dominating land force, and established new leadership, management and operational command systems.

The previous four general departments have been replaced by 15 functional organs under the CMC. Measures have been adopted to improve the leadership and management systems of the military branches.

The PLA has:

- established the PLAA leading organs;

调整武警部队领导指挥体制，中共中央和中央军委对武警部队实行集中统一领导，实行“中央军委—武警部队—部队”领导指挥体制。

建立健全联合作战指挥体制，健全军委联合作战指挥机构，组建战区联合作战指挥机构，成立5个战区，构建起“中央军委—战区—部队”的作战指挥体系。

建立健全法治监督体系，组建新的军委纪律检查委员会（军委监察委员会），组建新的军委政法委员会，组建军委审计署，形成决策权、执行权、监督权既相互制约又相互协调的权力运行体系。

- established the PLA Strategic Support Force (PLASSF);
- renamed the Second Artillery Force the PLARF; and
- established the PLAJLSF.

Thus, a CMC-Services-Troops leadership and management system has been put in place.

Changes have also been made to the PAP by adopting a CMC-PAP-Troops system to put the PAP under the centralized, unified leadership of the Party Central Committee and the CMC.

Measures to improve joint operations command system include improving the joint operations command organ of the CMC and establishing five TCs. A CMC-TCs-Troops command system is now in place.

Also important is the improvement of law-based supervision system. The Chinese military has established the CMC Discipline Inspection Commission (CMCDIC, also the CMC Supervision Commission, CMCSC), the CMC Political and Legal Affairs Commission (CMCPLC) and the CMC Audit Office (CMCAO). Thus, power is exercised in a way that decision-making, execution and supervision check each other and function in coordination.

军队规模结构和力量编成改革

规模结构和力量编成改革是推进军队组织形态现代化、构建中国特色现代军事力量体系的关键一步。按照调整优化结构、发展新型力量、理顺重大比例关系、压减数量规模的要求，推动军队由数量规模型向质量效能型、人力密集型向科技密集型转变。

调整军队规模比例，重塑力量结构布局。裁减军队员额30万，现役总员额减至200万。调整作战力量部署，形成与维护新时代国家安全需要相适应的战略布局。

调整作战部队编成，重构新型作战力量。陆军原18个集团军整合重组为13个集团军。在全军主要作战部队实行“军—旅—营”体制，推动部队编成向充实、合成、多能、灵活方向发展。

优化院校力量布局，重构军事科研体系。解放军和武警部队原有77所院校整合

Changes to Size, Structure, and Force Composition

Changing the size, structure, and force composition of the military is a key step in building a modern military that serves China's needs. Adjustments to the existing organizational structure include developing new types of forces, rebalancing the services, and reducing the total number of personnel, with a focus on improving quality and effectiveness and a transition from a personnel-intensive force to a technology-intensive one.

These changes have resulted in a reduction of 300,000 personnel, bringing the total headcount to two million. The deployment of combat forces has been adjusted in response to new strategic imperatives for defending national security.

As a result of the organizational reconfiguration, the original 18 army groups have been consolidated into 13, each with an army-brigade-battalion structure. Further changes aim to make the force composition complete, combined, multi-functional and flexible.

Reform also covers military educational and research institutions, resulting in the consolidation of 77 colleges operated by the PLA and the PAP into 44, and the

为44所，重塑国防大学、国防科技大学。成立军委军事科学研究指导委员会，调整组建新的军事科学院、军种研究院，形成以军事科学院为龙头、军兵种科研机构为骨干、院校和部队科研力量为辅助的军事科研力量布局。

reorganization of the National Defense University (NDU) and the National University of Defense Technology (NUDT). Other changes include the establishment of a CMC Military Research Steering Committee and the reorganization of the Academy of Military Science (AMS) and research institutes of various services. The military research network has been strengthened, comprising the AMS as the lead, the research institutes of the services and arms as the main forces, and the research components in educational institutions and the troops as supplements.

军事政策制度改革

坚持战斗力标准，着眼调动军事人员积极性、主动性、创造性，整体设计和推进军事政策制度改革，到2020年，完成各领域各系统主干政策制度改革，构建起中国特色社会主义军事政策制度体系基本框架；到2022年，健全各领域配套政策制度，构建起比较完备的中国特色社会主义军事政策制度体系。

主要包括：深化军队党的建设制度改革，维护党中央权威和集中统一领导，维护和贯彻军委主席负责制，确保党对人民军队的绝对领导；创新军事力量运用政策制度，有效保障全面履行新时代军队使命任务；重塑军事力量建设政策制度，推进建立军官职业化制度，优化军人待遇保障制度，健全军人荣誉体系，完善军事训练、装备发展、后勤建设、军事科研、国

Reform of Military Policies and Institutions

Reform of military policies and institutions is necessary to enhance combat capabilities and boost morale, innovation and creativity. By 2020, reform measures implemented across all areas will lead to a framework of military policies and institutions that reflects China's need to build socialism with Chinese characteristics. By 2022, the framework will be fleshed out to complete a coherent system of military policies and institutions.

Specifically, institutions for building stronger Party organizations in the military are under reform, aiming to ensure the authority and centralized, unified leadership of the Party Central Committee, the CMC chairperson responsibility system, and the Party's absolute leadership over the military. Revising policies on the employment of military forces is intended to better ensure that the military is effective in fulfilling its missions in the new era. Changes have to be made in this regard to boost the development of military forces, professionalize the officer corps, improve remuneration and other benefits for military personnel, and create mechanisms that ensure that service members are held in high regard. The reform should also help improve military training, equipment development, logistic support, military research, and national

防动员等方面政策制度，更好解放和发展战斗力；改革军事管理政策制度，提升军事系统运行效能，推动军队高质量发展。

defense mobilization, as part of the measures to develop combat capabilities. Upgraded military management with refined policies and institutions is important for efficient military systems and quality military development.

军委管总、战区主战、军种主建

2015年11月24日，习近平在中央军委改革工作会议上发表重要讲话，明确军委管总、战区主战、军种主建，是领导指挥体制改革的总原则。

军委管总，就是强化军委统一领导指挥全军的职能，完善军委战略管理和战略指挥功能，确保军委主席负责制有效落实。军委机关实行多部门制，作为军委的参谋机关、执行机关和服务机关，保障军委搞好顶层谋划、宏观指导、监察督导。

战区主战，就是战区作为联合作战指挥活动的重心和战略方向指挥的责任主体。重新划设5个战区，成立战区联合作战指挥机构，将军种有关指挥职能融入战区。

The Central Military Commission, Theater Commands, and Services

Addressing a CMC meeting on reform on November 24, 2015, Xi Jinping presented a general principle guiding the reform of the leadership and command system, affirming the CMC's overarching leadership role, the TCs' responsibility for military operations and the services' focus on developing capabilities.

The CMC's overall leadership ensures the CMC's unified command and leadership of the military, its strategic management and command, and the effective implementation of the CMC chairperson responsibility system. The CMC functional organs are responsible for providing advice, executing decisions, or providing other services to assist the CMC's overall planning, macro-level guidance, and oversight.

Theater commands are responsible for commanding joint operations across their areas of responsibility (AORs). There are now five TCs after the reorganization, each with its own joint operations command structure, which incorporates the command functions previously performed by the services.

Services are responsible for capability development and management of the troops

军种主建，就是军种作为建设管理活动的重心和本军种部队建设的责任主体。完善军种领导管理机构，将原军区有关建设管理职能交给军种。

under their respective command. The reform process involves improving the management structure of the services by transferring the capability development and management functions from the former MACs to the services.

中国特色社会主义军事制度

2017年10月18日，习近平在中国共产党第十九次全国代表大会的报告中提出，完善和发展中国特色社会主义军事制度。中国特色社会主义军事制度，是中国共产党为巩固党的执政地位和完善社会主义制度、维护国家安全和发展利益、促进世界和平与发展而确立的军事力量建设和运用规则体系，基本功能是调节军事关系、规范军事实践、保障军事发展，对国防和军队建设具有根本性、全局性、基础性作用。中国特色社会主义军事制度，是中国特色社会主义制度的重要组成部分，是中国共产党把马克思主义军事理论与中国军事实践相结合的伟大创新，是实现党在新时代的强军目标、全面建成世界一流军队的根本制度保障。

The Military System with Chinese Features

In his report to the 19th CPC National Congress, Xi Jinping called for developing and improving a military system with Chinese features, which is a system of institutions ensuring the CPC's position as the ruling party and its mission to improve the socialist system, protect national security and development interests, and promote world peace and development. The system guides the development and employment of the armed forces, and plays a fundamental and all-encompassing role in strengthening national defense and the military. An important component of China's socialist system, this system is a product of innovative application by the CPC of Marxist military theory to China's realities. At the institutional level it provides essential support for achieving the Party's goal of building a world-class military in the new era.

中国特色现代军事力量体系

2015年11月24日，习近平在中央军委改革工作会议上提出，努力构建能够打赢信息化战争、有效履行使命任务的中国特色现代军事力量体系。

主要包括：按照机动作战、立体攻防的战略要求，努力建设一支强大的现代化新型陆军；按照近海防御、远海防卫的战略要求，努力建设一支强大的现代化海军；按照空天一体、攻防兼备的战略要求，努力建设一支强大的现代化人民空军；按照核常兼备、全域慑战的战略要求，努力建设一支强大的现代化火箭军；按照体系融合、军民融合的战略要求，努力建设一支强大的现代化战略支援部队；按照联合作战、联合训练、联合保障的要求，努力建设一支强大的现代化联勤保障部队；按照多能一体、有效维稳的战略要求，努力建设一支强大的现代化武警部队。

The Modern Military Force Structure with Chinese Features

Addressing a CMC meeting on reform on November 24, 2015, Xi Jinping stressed the importance of building a modern military force structure with Chinese features, able to win informationized wars and effectively accomplish its missions.

To achieve this it is essential to build a modern army that meets the strategic demands for maneuver operations as well as multi-dimensional offense and defense; a modern navy capable of near seas defense and far seas protection; a modern air force that integrates air and space capabilities and coordinates offensive and defensive operations; a modern rocket force with both nuclear and conventional capabilities able to deter wars in all battle spaces; a modern strategic support force that integrates existing systems and aligns civil and military endeavors; a modern joint logistic support force that provides joint support for joint operations and joint training; and a modern armed police force that is distinguished by its versatility and effectiveness in the maintenance of stability.

联合作战指挥体系

2016年4月20日，习近平到军委联合作战指挥中心视察时强调，抓住改革机遇，锐意开拓创新，聚力攻坚克难，加快构建具有中国军队特色的联合作战指挥体系。实现这一目标任务，必须以党在新时代的强军目标为引领，贯彻新时代军事战略方针，建设绝对忠诚、善谋打仗、指挥高效、敢打必胜的联合作战指挥机构，构建平战一体、常态运行、专司主营、精干高效的战略战役指挥体系。

The Joint Operations Command System

While inspecting the CMC joint operations command center on April 20, 2016, Xi Jinping emphasized the need to build a joint operations command system that meets China's needs. He urged bold action to seize on the current reform momentum and overcome any barriers to realizing the goal. Efforts to this end must be guided by the Party's goal of building a strong military and the military strategic guideline for a new era. The reshuffled command system must be placed under the absolute leadership of the Party. It must be able to command with courage, efficiency, and confidence. A capable and efficient joint operations command system is to be built, which is composed of permanent and specialized command establishments for both peacetime and wartime operations.

战区

战区是本战略方向的唯一最高联合作战指挥机构，按照平战一体、常态运行、专司主营、精干高效的要求，履行联合作战指挥职能，担负应对本战略方向安全威胁、维护和平、遏制战争、打赢战争的使命。

2016年2月1日，习近平向各战区授予军旗并发布训令，中国人民解放军新的战区正式成立。新的战区划设为东部战区、南部战区、西部战区、北部战区、中部战区。重新调整划设战区，组建战区联合作战指挥机构，是全面实施改革强军战略的标志性举措，是构建联合作战体系的历史性进展，对确保人民军队能打仗、打胜仗，有效维护国家安全，具有重大而深远的意义。

Theater Commands

Theater commands are the sole and highest-ranking joint operations command organizations across their respective AOR. Measures have been adopted to build the TCs into permanent, specialized and streamlined ones able to command joint operations in both peacetime and wartime. It is their duty to counter security threats across their AORs, maintain peace, and deter, fight and win wars.

On February 1, 2016, Xi Jinping handed the command flags over to respective TC commanders, marking the formal establishment of the new commands, namely the Eastern, Southern, Western, Northern and Central theater commands. Measures to put in place the TCs and the theater-level command establishments represent an important milestone in defense reform and a giant step toward the creation of a joint operations system. The consequent growth of capabilities will enable the military to better protect national security and prevail in the battlefield.

军官职业化制度

2013年11月，中国共产党十八届三中全会《决定》提出，以建立军官职业化制度为牵引，逐步形成科学规范的军队干部制度体系。2018年11月，习近平在中央军委政策制度改革工作会议上，对建立军官职业化制度作出具体部署，明确以专业化为核心，牢固确立战斗力这个唯一的根本的标准，强化打仗能力导向，以军衔主导的军官等级制度为重点，构建军官培养、选拔、服役、待遇等各项制度，构建军官岗位分类制度，调整军官服役制度，创新军官职业发展管理制度，统筹设计军官培训、考核、晋升、任用、交流等制度。

Career Officers System

Since the outcome document of the Third Plenary Session of the 18th CPC Central Committee was unveiled, a new military officer management system has gradually taken shape, spurred by a professionalization process.

Addressing a CMC conference on policy reform in November 2018, Xi Jinping outlined a career plan for military officers, calling for professionalization of the officer corps as a key to bolstering the military's capabilities. Measures include the introduction of a military hierarchy based on ranks, the update of institutions on officer training, selection, service, compensation and benefits schemes, and the classification of military specialties. Also critical to an innovative military career development system is an integrated approach to managing officer training, evaluation, promotion, appointment and exchange programs.

文职人员制度

文职人员是现代军队的重要人力资源。2017年9月，国务院、中央军委公布施行新修订的《中国人民解放军文职人员条例》，将文职人员列为军队人员的重要组成部分，建立与国家公务员和事业单位工作人员制度相衔接、具有比较优势的文职人员管理和保障制度。2018年7月，中国军队首次面向社会公开招考文职人员。实行文职人员制度，是推进军事人力资源政策制度改革的重大创新，对优化军事力量构成、提高军事人力资源开发使用效益意义重大。

Civilian Personnel in the Military

Civilian personnel are an important source of military manpower, and an integral part of the PLA, as per the Regulations on Civilian Personnel in the Military as revised in September 2017. The regulations provide for a civilian personnel management system, including civilian personnel compensation and benefits schemes, which corresponds to and compares favorably with the national civil service and public institutions.

The military's first-ever recruitment examination for civilian personnel open to the public was held in July 2018. The use of civilians in the military attests to progress in reforming the military's human resource policies, and contributes significantly to improving the military's personnel composition and development.

退役军人管理保障

退役军人是党和国家的宝贵财富。新中国成立后，解放军和武警部队先后有5700余万人退出现役。退役军人管理保障，主要包括褒扬彰显退役军人为党、国家和人民牺牲奉献的精神风范和价值导向，军队转业干部、复员干部、退休干部、退役士兵的移交安置工作和自主择业退役军人服务管理、待遇保障工作，退役军人教育培训、优待抚恤等工作，全国拥军优属工作，烈士及退役军人荣誉奖励、军人公墓维护以及纪念活动。习近平在中国共产党第十九次全国代表大会的报告中强调，组建退役军人管理保障机构，维护军人军属合法权益，让军人成为全社会尊崇的职业。按照中国共产党十九届三中全

Veteran Affairs Management and Veteran Support

Veterans are valuable to the Party and the state. Since the founding of the People's Republic in 1949, 57 million people have been demobilized from the PLA and the PAP. Veteran affairs management and veteran support include:

- development of a culture that holds veterans in high regard and rewards them for their dedication and contribution to the Party, the nation and the people;
- assistance to demobilized or retired officers and honorably discharged military personnel to ensure their smooth transition to civilian life, including provision of job placement services, assistance with choosing jobs, and benefits support services;
- education, occupational training, preferential policies, compensation and benefits management;
- engagements by government agencies at all levels to support the military and military families; and
- military family and military service appreciation and award programs, maintenance of military cemeteries, and organization of commemoration events.

会《决定》和中华人民共和国十三届全国人大一次会议批准的国务院机构改革方案，2018年3月组建退役军人事务部，作为国务院组成部门。这对建立健全集中统一、职责清晰的退役军人管理保障体制具有重要意义。

In his report to the 19th CPC National Congress, Xi Jinping emphasized the importance of establishing veteran support mechanisms and protecting the legitimate rights and interests of military personnel and their families to ensure that military careers are respected in society.

In accordance with the outcome document of the Third Plenary Session of the 19th CPC Central Committee and the State Council organizational reform plan adopted by the 13th NPC at its first session, the Ministry of Veterans Affairs was established under the State Council in March 2018. The move is key to creating a unified veteran support system with well-defined responsibilities.

军队法治建设

军队法治建设，主要包括军事立法、军事执法、军事司法、军事守法普法等各领域的建设活动，涉及军队建设发展方方面面。深入推进新时代军队法治建设，必须紧紧围绕党在新时代的强军目标，着眼全面加强革命化现代化正规化建设，坚持党对人民军队的绝对领导，坚持战斗力标准，坚持官兵主体地位，坚持依法和从严相统一，坚持法治建设和思想政治建设相结合，创新发展依法治军理论和实践，构建完善的中国特色军事法治体系，提高国防和军队建设法治化水平。

Governing the Military in Accordance with Law

Measures to strengthen law-based governance over the military include, *inter alia*, development of military laws, law enforcement, implementation of the military justice system, and legal awareness training. These measures are implemented to support the Party's goal of building a strong military in the new era, with a view to strengthening the military's political ethics, modernization initiatives, and organizational structure. They contribute to ensuring the Party's absolute leadership over the military and the development of the military's combat capabilities. Implementation of these measures relies on all service members. Compliance with laws and regulations is enhanced through appropriate enforcement mechanisms. Promotion of the rule of law within the military goes in tandem with political ethics education, theoretical development and practices applicable to a military context to put in place an updated military legal system with Chinese features and strengthen the military's law-based fabric.

中国特色军事法治体系

中国特色军事法治体系，包括军事法规制度体系、军事法治实施体系、军事法治监督体系、军事法治保障体系。构建完善中国特色军事法治体系，必须用党在新时代的强军目标审视和引领军事立法，提高军事法规制度的针对性、系统性、操作性；必须明确执法责任，完善执法制度，健全依法运转的工作机制；必须综合运用党内监督、层级监督、专门监督、群众监督、社会监督，形成严密有效的监督体系；必须加强军事法治理论建设、军事法律人才队伍建设、军事法治文化建设。

The Military Legal System with Chinese Features

China's unique military legal system consists of a set of laws and regulations applicable to the military, along with enforcement mechanisms, oversight mechanisms, and legal protection and support services. The system must be guided by the Party's goal of building a strong military in the new era. Measures include:

- developing a systematic and enforceable legal framework specifically relevant to the military;
- developing accountability mechanisms, strengthening law enforcement and improving procedures of law-based governance;
- coordinating oversight functions, including inner-Party oversight functions, the military's oversight mechanisms at different levels, and public scrutiny, to ensure effectiveness; and
- developing theories, professionals, and a cultural environment in favor of an enhanced military legal system.

治军方式根本性转变

依法治军、从严治军是强军之基，是中国共产党建军治军的基本方略。深入推进依法治军、从严治军，要求治军方式发生一场深刻变革，实现从单纯依靠行政命令的做法向依法行政的根本性转变，从单纯靠习惯和经验开展工作的方式向依靠法规和制度开展工作的根本性转变，从突击式、运动式抓工作的方式向按条令条例办事的根本性转变。近年来，中国军队科学设置机构，建立职责清单，强化官兵法治素养，军队建设、管理和作战行动日益标准化、规范化、精细化，全军逐步形成党委依法决策、机关依法指导、部队依法行动、官兵依法履职的良好局面。

A Fundamental Change to How the Military Is Run

Effective and strict implementation of law-based governance underpins the effort to build a strong military, and constitutes the central pillar of the CPC's strategy for strengthening the armed forces. This requires a fundamental change to the way the military is run, that is, a paradigm shift from reliance on experience and administrative orders to law-based processes, and from ad hoc, stop-gap and improvised measures to a consistent and systematic approach that respects established codes and procedures.

Efforts to this end in recent years have focused on better delegation of responsibilities in the reformed organizations; rollout of lists of duties; legal awareness training; and targeted approaches to the development, management and employment of military forces in accordance with standards and regulations. This is designed to ensure that all Party committees, executive branches, military units and service members act in compliance with established rules.

全面推进基层建设

基层是部队全部工作和战斗力的基础。2015年1月，习近平视察驻昆明部队时指出，要坚持扭住党的组织抓基层，扭住战备训练抓基层，扭住官兵主体抓基层，扭住厉行法治抓基层。2019年11月，习近平在中央军委基层建设会议上强调，全面锻造听党话、跟党走的过硬基层，能打仗、打胜仗的过硬基层，法纪严、风气正的过硬基层，为推进强军事业提供坚实基础和支撑。

按照《军队基层建设纲要》全面推进基层建设，主要包括：在基层党组织建设上用劲，提高解决自身问题、领导部队全面建设和带领官兵遂行任务的能力，增强党组织创造力、凝聚力、战斗力；围绕战备训练开展基层工作，深入开展岗位练兵、比武竞赛等活动，加强战斗精神培育，营造练兵打仗的浓厚氛围；尊重官兵主体地位和首创精神，加强部队政治民主、经济民主、军事民主“三大民主”建

A Focus on Primary-Level Units

Primary-level units are the military's bedrock. While inspecting troops stationed in Kunming of Yunnan Province in January 2015, Xi Jinping reaffirmed the need to strengthen primary-level units with focus on their Party organizations, combat readiness, military training, personnel development, and implementation of rules and regulations. Addressing a CMC meeting in November 2019, Xi Jinping emphasized the importance of improving the quality of the primary-level units in areas including political awareness and loyalty to the Party, combat skills and abilities, legal compliance, and moral integrity, so as to provide a solid basis for building a strong military.

The Outlines on Strengthening Primary-level Military Units call for:

- strengthening Party organizations at the primary level, by addressing issues faced by these organizations, especially strengthening their effectiveness and ability to generate innovative ideas and mobilize efforts around the Party's objectives;
- stepping up military training, including function-specific training and organization of combat skills contests, cultivating a strong fighting spirit, and developing

设，增强基层内生动力和工作主动性，紧紧依靠官兵把基层建设好；按照条令条例规范基层建设，狠抓经常性思想工作和经常性管理工作落实，营造风清气正的良好环境，把依法治军作为基层建设的基本方式确立起来，保持部队正规秩序和安全稳定。

an inspiring military culture;

- building a sense of ownership among all service members and promoting democratic practices in all aspects of military life to encourage the rank and file to realize their full potential; and
- strengthening compliance with rules and regulations and political ethics education at the primary level to create an environment that rewards integrity, and implementing law-based governance measures to build well-disciplined and stable troops.

总体国家安全观

2019年10月，中国共产党十九届四中全会《决定》提出，坚持总体国家安全观，以人民安全为宗旨，以政治安全为根本，以经济安全为基础，以军事、科技、文化、社会安全为保障，健全国家安全体系，增强国家安全能力。总体国家安全观要求：既重视外部安全，又重视内部安全，对内求发展、求变革、求稳定、建设平安中国，对外求和平、求合作、求共赢、建设和谐世界；既重视国土安全，又重视国民安全，坚持以民为本、以人为本，坚持国家安全一切为了人民、一切依靠人民，真正夯实国家安全的群众基础；既重视传统安全，又重视非传统安全，构建集政治安全、国土安全、军事安全、经济安全、文化安全、社会安全、科技安

A Holistic Approach to National Security

In the decision made at its fourth plenary session in October 2019, the 19th Central Committee of the CPC emphasized the need to take a holistic approach to national security. Through this approach, a full spectrum of security issues is assessed. The people's security is taken as a prioritized mission, political security as a fundamental task, economic security as the foundation, and military, scientific, technological, cultural and public security as factors enabling the full-fledged framework and capabilities of national security.

This holistic approach calls for a focus on both internal and external security. Internally, it is essential to promote development, continue reform, maintain stability, and create a safe environment. Externally, we should promote international peace, seek cooperation and mutual benefit, and strive to bring harmony to the world.

Homeland security and the security of our citizens are both of paramount importance. All initiatives taken in this respect will be people-centered and implemented for the people, on the basis of the people's needs, and with the support of the people. Security issues, both traditional and non-traditional, will be taken into account. The

全、信息安全、生态安全、资源安全、核安全等于一体的国家安全体系；既重视发展问题，又重视安全问题，发展是安全的基础，安全是发展的条件；既重视自身安全，又重视共同安全，打造命运共同体，推动各方朝着互利互惠、共同安全的目标相向而行。

national security system we envisage will integrate political security, homeland security, military security, economic security, cultural security, public security, scientific and technological security, information security, eco-environmental security, resources security, and nuclear security.

Development issues will be considered in tandem with security issues. Development provides a basis for security, whereas security constitutes a necessary condition for development. Our national security must also be viewed in the context of international security. For the sake of the international community and our shared future, we should all work toward our goal of satisfying the world's security needs in a way that is beneficial to all.

共同、综合、合作、可持续的安全观

2014年5月，在亚信上海峰会上，习近平首次倡议树立共同、综合、合作、可持续的亚洲安全观，走出一条共建共享共赢的亚洲安全之路。亚洲安全观提出后，得到大多数国家的支持，它彻底摆脱了冷战思维，是新型的安全理念。

共同，就是尊重和保障每一个国家的安全，不能一个国家安全而其他国家不安全、一部分国家安全而另一部分国家不安全，更不能牺牲别国安全谋求自身的所谓绝对安全。综合，就是统筹维护传统领域安全和非传统领域安全，通盘考虑安全问题的历史经纬和现实状况，多管齐下、综合施策，协调推进世界安全治理。合作，就是通过对话合作促进各国各地区安全，增进战略互信，以合作谋和平、以合作促

A Common, Comprehensive, Cooperative, and Sustainable Security Concept

At the 2014 Shanghai Summit of the Conference on Interaction and Confidence-building Measures in Asia (CICA), Xi Jinping introduced a concept for Asian security that emphasizes a common, comprehensive, cooperative, and sustainable approach, one that aims through joint efforts to provide a secure future in the region enjoyed by all. Supported by most countries, this concept represents new thinking that rejects any Cold-War mentality.

A focus on common security means that the security needs of every country should be respected and met. No country or group of countries should pursue absolute national security at the expense of others. To address both traditional and non-traditional security challenges at the global level, we need a comprehensive, multi-pronged strategy that takes into account historical perspectives and current realities. Cooperation and dialog are indispensable to strengthening the security of individual countries as well as regional security. They serve as useful strategic confidence-building measures in the quest for

安全，以和平方式解决争端。可持续，就是坚持发展和安全并重以实现持久安全，聚焦发展主题，积极改善民生，缩小贫富差距，不断夯实安全根基。

2017年1月18日，习近平在瑞士日内瓦“共商共筑人类命运共同体”高级别会议上，发表题为《共同构建人类命运共同体》的主旨演讲，强调坚持共建共享，建设一个普遍安全的世界，提出各方应该树立共同、综合、合作、可持续的安全观。共同、综合、合作、可持续的安全观，是在总结第二次世界大战后特别是21世纪以来人类社会在国际安全、国际政治、国际战略问题上的经验教训基础上提出的中国方案，是站在构建可持续发展与可持续安全的人类命运共同体的高度提出的重要思想，也是对和平共处五项原则的继承和发展，是中国对世界和平与安全的重要贡献。

peace and for resolution of conflicts through peaceful means. Sustainable security is possible only when security measures are implemented in conjunction with sustained development efforts to improve the wellbeing of the people and narrow the gap between the rich and the poor as part of the strategy to address the root causes of security risks.

In his keynote speech at a high-level meeting in Geneva, Switzerland, in January 2017, Xi Jinping laid out a vision for a global community with a shared future. Highlighting the importance of consultation and joint efforts, he presented a common, comprehensive, cooperative, and sustainable security concept. Based on the experience and lessons learned in addressing global security, political and strategic issues since the Second World War, and especially since the dawn of the 21st century, this concept is key to building a global community with a shared future that promotes sustainable development and lasting security. It builds on and enriches the Five Principles of Peaceful Coexistence, and represents China's contribution to world peace and security.

新时代中国防御性国防政策

中国的社会主义国家性质，走和平发展道路的战略抉择，独立自主的和平外交政策，“和为贵”的中华文化传统，决定了中国始终不渝奉行防御性国防政策。坚决捍卫国家主权、安全、发展利益，是新时代中国国防的根本目标。坚持永不称霸、永不扩张、永不谋求势力范围，是新时代中国国防的鲜明特征。贯彻落实新时代军事战略方针，是新时代中国国防的战略指导。坚持走中国特色强军之路，是新时代中国国防的发展路径。服务构建人类命运共同体，是新时代中国国防的世界意义。

A National Defense Policy in the New Era That Is Defensive in Nature

The socialist system of China, the strategic decision to follow the path of peaceful development, the independent foreign policy of peace, and the best of cultural traditions – considering peace and harmony as fundamentals – determine that China will pursue a national defense policy that is defensive in nature. China's national defense policy in the new era breaks down as follows:

- Fundamental goal: Resolutely safeguarding China's sovereignty, security and development interests;
- Distinctive feature: Never seeking hegemony, expansion or spheres of influence;
- Strategic guidance: The military strategic guideline for a new era;
- Path forward: Strengthening the military in the Chinese way; and
- Global significance: Serving the building of a global community with a shared future.

永不称霸、永不扩张、永不谋求势力范围

坚持永不称霸、永不扩张、永不谋求势力范围，是新时代中国国防的鲜明特征。

中华民族历来爱好和平。近代以来，中国人民饱受侵略和战乱之苦，深感和平之珍贵、发展之迫切，决不会把自己经受过的悲惨遭遇强加于人。新中国成立70年来，中国没有主动挑起过任何一场战争和冲突。改革开放以来，中国致力于促进世界和平，主动裁减军队员额400余万。中国由积贫积弱发展成为世界第二大经济体，靠的不是别人的施舍，更不是军事扩张和殖民掠夺，而是人民勤劳、维护和平。中国既通过维护世界和平为自身发展

A Pledge Never to Pursue Hegemony, Expansion or Spheres of Influence

China's national defense policy is most prominently characterized by a pledge never to pursue hegemony, expansion or spheres of influence.

From the mid-19th century to the founding of the People's Republic in 1949, China was ravaged by foreign aggression and civil wars. The Chinese people cherish peace, understand the imperative for national development, and will never impose on others the sufferings inflicted on us. China has never provoked a war or conflict over the 70 years since 1949. We have remained committed to world peace and voluntarily reduced our forces by more than four million since the start of China's reform and opening up in the late 1970s.

Instead of benefiting from the largesse of others, or riding on the back of military expansionism or the plundering of colonies, China's successful transition from a poor and weak country to the world's second largest economy relies on a hard-working people and their unrelenting quest for peace. Efforts to maintain world peace help create conditions conducive to national development. Progress

创造有利条件，又通过自身发展促进世界和平，真诚希望所有国家都选择和平发展道路，共同防范冲突和战争。

中国坚持在和平共处五项原则基础上发展同各国的友好合作，尊重各国人民自主选择发展道路的权利，主张通过平等对话和谈判协商解决国际争端，反对干涉别国内政，反对恃强凌弱，反对把自己的意志强加于人。中国坚持结伴不结盟，不参加任何军事集团，反对侵略扩张，反对动辄使用武力或以武力相威胁。中国的国防建设和发展，始终着眼于满足自身安全的正当需要，始终是世界和平力量的增长。历史已经并将继续证明，中国决不走追逐霸权、“国强必霸”的老路。无论将来发展到哪一步，中国都不会威胁谁，都不会谋求建立势力范围。

in national development, for its part, also contributes to world peace. We sincerely hope that all countries will choose peaceful development, and work together to prevent conflict and war.

China seeks cooperation with others on the basis of the Five Principles of Peaceful Coexistence, and respects other countries' right to decide how they will develop. International disputes should be resolved through dialog and consultation between the countries concerned on an equal footing. China stands firm against interference in other countries' internal affairs, bullying of the weak by the powerful, and any attempt to impose one's own will on others.

China seeks partnership rather than alliances with some against others. It has never joined any military bloc and are firmly opposed to any aggression or expansionist moves, and any wanton use or threat of force. China's defense capability responds to its own legitimate security needs, and contributes to world peace.

History has proven and will continue to prove that China will never follow the beaten track of big powers in seeking hegemony. No matter how far we progress, we will never threaten anyone, or seek spheres of influence.

中国的核政策

中国始终奉行在任何时候和任何情况下都不首先使用核武器、无条件不对无核武器国家和无核武器区使用或威胁使用核武器的核政策，主张最终全面禁止和彻底销毁核武器，不会与任何国家进行核军备竞赛，始终把自身核力量维持在国家安全需要的最低水平。中国坚持自卫防御核战略，目的是遏制他国对中国使用或威胁使用核武器，确保国家战略安全。

China's Nuclear Policy

China is always committed to a nuclear policy of no first use of nuclear weapons at any time and under any circumstances, and unconditionally no use of or threat to use nuclear weapons against non-nuclear-weapon states or nuclear-weapon-free zones. China advocates the ultimate complete prohibition and destruction of nuclear weapons, does not engage in any nuclear arms race with any other country, and keeps its nuclear capabilities at the minimum level required for national security. China's nuclear strategy focuses on self-defense, and aims to ensure the strategic security of the country by deterring the potential threat or use of nuclear weapons by others against China.

理性、协调、并进的核安全观

中国是世界上第一个正式提出核安全观的国家。2014年3月24日，在荷兰海牙举行的第三届核安全峰会上，习近平发表重要讲话，首次全面阐述了理性、协调、并进的核安全观。主要内容可以概括为四句话：一是发展和安全并重，以确保安全为前提发展核能事业。二是权利和义务并重，以尊重各国权益为基础推进国际核安全进程。三是自主和协作并重，以互利共赢为途径寻求普遍核安全。四是治标和治本并重，以消除根源为目标全面推进核安全努力。中国承诺，为实现持久核安全，愿意继续作出自己的努力和贡献。

A Rational, Coordinated, and Balanced Approach to Nuclear Security

Addressing the Third Nuclear Security Summit in the Hague on March 24, 2014, Xi Jinping outlined for the first time a rational, coordinated, and balanced approach to nuclear security. It places equal emphasis on:

(a) development and security, to ensure safety and security in the development of nuclear energy;

(b) rights and obligations of all countries, as far as international nuclear security is concerned;

(c) independent projects and collaborative efforts, to ensure nuclear security for all; and

(d) short-term measures and long-term solutions, the latter being aimed at removing associated risks at source.

As the first country to propose such an approach, China is committed to making continued efforts to achieve lasting nuclear security.

国际军事合作

开展军事交流与合作，是中国《国防法》的明确规定。国际军事合作是指中国与外国为了谋求各自或共同的战略利益，在军事领域开展的联合行动与相互交流、协作配合。国际军事合作是党和国家对外工作的重要组成部分，是国防和军队建设的重要领域。国际军事合作的主要方式包括：防务安全对话磋商，国际反恐等联合军事行动，联合军事演习训练，军事装备技术合作，人员交流互访，国际军备控制，提供维和、护航、人道主义援助救灾等国际公共安全产品，等等。中国军队坚持共同、综合、合作、可持续的安全观，通过广泛的国际军事合作发展不结盟、不对抗、不针对第三方的军事关系，推动建

International Military Cooperation

Military cooperation and exchanges are authorized by China's National Defense Law. China's military cooperation with other countries is intended to further our respective and shared strategic interests through joint operations, exchanges and collaboration. It is an important element of foreign engagements of the Party and the state, and an important area of defense and military development. Areas of cooperation include:

- security dialog and consultation;
- joint international military operations including counter-terrorism operations;
- joint military exercises and training;
- military equipment and technology cooperation;
- personnel exchanges;
- international arms control; and
- providing international public security goods, including UN peacekeeping operations, naval escort missions, and humanitarian assistance and disaster relief (HADR) operations.

China's military is committed to a common, comprehensive, cooperative, and sustainable security concept. Its extensive international military cooperation is intended to build foreign military relations featuring non-alliance and non-confrontation that target

立公平有效的集体安全机制和军事互信机制，积极拓展军事安全合作空间，营造有利于国家和平发展的安全环境，维护世界和平与地区稳定。中国军队不断探索与世界各国军队合作的新领域、新内容、新模式，“朋友圈”越来越大，构建起全方位、宽领域、多层次的国际军事合作新格局。

no third party. It aims to create fair and effective collective security and mutual trust mechanisms. Expanding military and security cooperation helps create a safe and secure environment conducive to national peaceful development and contributes to world peace and regional stability.

China's military will continue to explore new areas and new formats of collaboration with other militaries, make more friends, and strengthen cooperation at all levels.

构建新型安全伙伴关系

2018年10月举行的第八届北京香山论坛，主题为“打造平等互信、合作共赢的新型安全伙伴关系”。构建新型安全伙伴关系，是顺应时代发展潮流提出的国际安全治理新理念。主要内容包括：提倡对话不对抗，结伴不结盟，多边不单边，互利合作而不搞零和博弈；通过多形式、多层次、多渠道加强与各国及其军队的对话交流，增信释疑，逐步建立军事安全互信机制；坚持以对话磋商妥善处理矛盾分歧，有效管控战略风险，携手应对各种威胁挑战，共同为维护地区和世界的和平稳定作出努力。

构建新型安全伙伴关系，旨在倡导各国跳出结盟或对抗的窠臼，顺应时代发展

A New Type of Security Partnership

The Eighth Beijing Xiangshan Forum was held in October 2018 under the theme "Building a New Type of Security Partnership of Equality, Mutual Trust and Win-Win Cooperation." The new-type security partnership is a new approach to international security governance responding to the development of the times.

The approach calls for dialog rather than confrontation, collaboration rather than alliance with some against others, multilateralism rather than unilateralism, and mutually beneficial cooperation rather than zero-sum games. It requires expanded exchanges with other countries and their militaries in various formats, at different levels and through multiple channels to build mutual understanding and trust. It adheres to resolving disputes and differences through dialog and consultation, effective control of risks, and joint actions to counter threats and security challenges and contribute to world and regional peace and stability.

The goal of building a new type of security partnership is to encourage all countries to free themselves from the straitjacket of old thinking of alliance or confrontation, and embrace an inclusive and constructive approach to developing security

潮流，平等相待、互商互谅，探索构建不设假想敌、不针对第三方、具有包容性和建设性的安全伙伴关系，推动构建人类命运共同体，呼吁各国共担责任，共同走出一条共建、共享、共赢的安全合作之路，促进构建相互尊重、公平正义、合作共赢的新型国际关系，共创人类更加美好的未来。

partnerships on the basis of equality and mutual understanding – partnerships that accommodate today's trends and do not target an assumed enemy or any third party. It is essential to promote the building of a global community with a shared future, and call on all countries to shoulder their responsibilities and work together to strengthen security cooperation that benefits all, to forge a new form of international relations featuring mutual respect, fairness, justice, and win-win cooperation, and to create a better future for humanity.

军事互信

军事互信是维护国家安全发展和地区和平稳定的有效途径，包括加强沟通与理解，设置军事限制，对协议遵守情况进行监督和检查等。中国坚持以增强政治互信为基础，以促进共同安全为目标，遵循平等协商、尊重彼此核心利益和重大安全关切、不针对第三国、不威胁和损害他国安全稳定等原则，推动建立平等、互利、有效的军事互信机制。通过战略磋商与对话、边境建立信任措施、海上安全对话与合作、地区安全合作、对外军事交往等，全方位发展对外军事关系，努力营造互信互利的军事安全环境。

Military Mutual Confidence

Building military mutual confidence contributes to national security and development, and promotes regional peace and stability, *inter alia* by strengthening communication and mutual understanding, setting limits on military activities, and monitoring and verifying compliance with agreements in force.

China is committed to building equal-footed, mutually beneficial and effective military mutual confidence mechanisms on the basis of enhanced political mutual trust, with a view to strengthening security for all countries. Such mechanisms should observe equality, respect for each other's core interests and major security concerns, and the principles of not targeting any third country, and not threatening or undermining other countries' security and stability.

Greater efforts will be made to strengthen strategic consultation and dialog, establish confidence-building measures in the border areas, enhance maritime security dialog and cooperation, boost regional security cooperation, and expand exchanges with other militaries, so as to develop all-dimensional foreign military relations and create a military security setting featuring mutual trust and mutual benefit.

军备控制

军备控制，是指国家或国际组织通过双边或多边国际条约对武器系统的研究、试验、生产、部署、使用及转让或军队规模等进行的限制，目的在于减轻军事存在的危险性和一旦战争爆发时进行相对的克制。

中国重视并积极参与国际军备控制进程，主张充分发挥联合国及其他相关国际组织和多边机制作用，巩固和加强现有多边军控、裁军和防扩散体系，尊重和照顾各国正当合理安全关切，维护全球战略平衡和稳定。在核裁军方面，中国一贯主张全面禁止和彻底销毁核武器。在防扩散方面，中国坚决反对大规模杀伤性武器及其运载工具扩散，参加了防扩散领域所有的国际条约和相关国际组织。在禁止化学、生物武器方面，中国认真履行《禁止化学武器公约》《禁止生物武器公约》的各项义务，建立了相应的履约机制。在防止外

Arms Control

Arms control is exercised by countries or international organizations through bilateral or multilateral treaties to restrict the development, testing, production, deployment, use or transfer of weaponry systems, or to put a limit on the size of militaries, in order to reduce any risk associated with military presence, and put the use of force under restrictions in case of war.

China attaches great importance to and actively participates in global arms control process, supports the crucial role of the United Nations, other international organizations and multilateral mechanisms in global arms control, and calls for efforts to strengthen existing multilateral arms control, disarmament and nonproliferation regimes. China endeavors to accommodate other countries' legitimate security concerns and maintain global strategic balance and stability.

On nuclear disarmament, China always advocates the complete prohibition and destruction of nuclear weapons. With respect to nonproliferation, China stands firm against the spread of weapons of mass destruction and their delivery systems, and participates in all international treaties on nonproliferation and related international organizations.

On prohibition of chemical and biological weapons, China is fully committed to the obligations under the Chemical

空军备竞赛方面，中国政府一贯主张和平利用外空，反对外空武器化和外空军备竞赛。在常规武器军控方面，中国严格履行《特定常规武器公约》及其议定书规定的各项义务，按要求提交公约及其所附《地雷议定书》年度履约报告。在军费透明和常规武器转让登记方面，中国从2007年起参加联合国军费透明制度，同年起恢复参加联合国常规武器登记册并提交年度报告，致力于增进与世界各国的军事互信。此外，中国始终将军队的数量和规模控制在维护国家安全需要的最低限度，多次主动采取单方面的裁军行动。

Weapons Convention and the Biological Weapons Convention and has established corresponding implementation mechanisms. With regard to prevention of arms race in outer space, the Chinese government calls for peaceful use of outer space, and is opposed to its militarization and any arms race there.

On conventional weapons control, China strictly abides by its obligations under the Convention on Certain Conventional Weapons and its protocols, including submission of annual national reports reviewing its efforts to implement the Convention and its Protocol on Mines, Booby-traps and Other Devices.

Regarding transparency in military spending and registration of transfers of conventional arms, China joined the UN Standardized Instrument for Reporting Military Expenditures in 2007 and resumed submission of annual reports to the UN Register of Conventional Arms the same year in an effort to build trust among countries.

Moreover, China always keeps the scale of its military to the minimum level required for national security, and has taken the initiative to cut its armed forces several times.

军事援助

中国作为一个发展中国家，多年来在致力于自身国防和军队建设发展的同时，始终坚持承担相应国际义务，向经济困难的其他发展中国家提供力所能及的军事援助。相互尊重、平等相待、重信守诺、互利共赢是中国军事援助遵循的基本原则，主要形式有装备援助、专家派出、人员培训等。中国提供军事援助，坚持不附带任何政治条件、不干涉受援国内政，坚持帮助受援国提高军事安全和军队自主发展能力，坚持在防务领域的平等互利、共同发展，坚持量力而行、尽力而为，坚持与时俱进、改革创新，注重塑造有利的地区安全格局。

Military Assistance

As a developing country, China always fulfills its international obligations and extends military assistance to other developing countries in need of such assistance, while enhancing its own defense capability. China's military assistance is based on the principle of mutual respect, equality, trust, and mutual benefit. It includes, *inter alia*, provision of equipment, expert missions, and personnel training. China provides assistance without imposing any extraneous political conditions and without interfering in the internal affairs of recipient countries. Rather, the assistance is designed to help recipient countries enhance their security and develop their own military capabilities. We do what we can within our ability to promote shared prosperity, and tailor our military assistance to today's specific needs in an innovative manner with a focus on strengthening regional security.

维护海外利益

海外利益是中国国家利益的重要组成部分。中国通过构建海外利益安全工作体系，综合运用政治、经济、外交、军事等手段，保障海外本国公民、机构、资产、能源资源、战略通道安全，维护国际形象，塑造有利国际态势。中国维护海外利益，不追求一己私利，注重把自身利益与各国人民的共同利益统一起来，致力于为国际社会提供公共安全产品。

近年来，中国海外利益面临多样化安全威胁，特别是因当地战争或内乱而遭受威胁和损失的情况不断发生，维护海外利益安全已凸显为关系国计民生的重大战略议题。中国军队积极推动国际安全和军事合作，完善海外利益保护机制。着眼弥补海外行动和保障能力差距，发展远洋力量，建设海外补给点，增强遂行多样化军事任务能力。实施海上护航，维护海上战

Protection of Overseas Interests

China's overseas interests are an important part of its national interests. It is important to have in place a framework that integrates political, economic, diplomatic, and military measures to protect China's overseas interests, including its citizens, entities and assets, its energy resources, and the security of strategic passageways, and protect its international image and help create a more secure world. To this end China seeks to align the protection of Chinese interests abroad with the protection of interests shared by all, and to contribute more public security goods to the international community.

In recent years, China's overseas interests have been exposed to a diverse array of security threats, especially local conflicts and unrest. Protection of these interests has become a strategic issue that bears on the wellbeing of the people and the development of the country. China's military seeks increased international security cooperation to better protect Chinese interests abroad. Measures to this end also aim to identify and address inadequacies in overseas operations and support, and develop ocean-going naval forces, overseas supply facilities, and the military's ability to perform diversified tasks, including naval escorts, protection of

略通道安全，遂行海上维权、撤离海外中国公民等行动。2015年3月，也门安全局势严重恶化，中国海军护航编队赴也门亚丁湾海域，首次直接靠泊交战区域港口，安全撤离621名中国公民和279名来自巴基斯坦、埃塞俄比亚、新加坡、意大利、波兰、德国、加拿大、英国、印度、日本等15个国家的公民。

strategic maritime passageways, maintaining China's maritime interests, and evacuation of Chinese nationals.

In March 2015 when the security situation in Yemen deteriorated, China's naval frigates deployed in the region for naval escort missions successfully evacuated from Yemen's port of Aden 621 Chinese citizens and 279 foreign nationals from 15 countries, including Pakistan, Ethiopia, Singapore, Italy, Poland, Germany, Canada, the UK, India, and Japan, in a first-ever action in an overseas conflict zone.

维护新型安全领域利益

新型安全领域，是相对于传统领域而言、引领时代潮流的新兴安全空间，具有鲜明的时代特征，主要包括太空、网络、人工智能、生物等领域，是当前科学技术发展应用最活跃的新领域，是人类未来生存发展的新领域，是维护国家安全的新领域。维护新型安全领域利益，应秉持共同开发、共同利用、共同管理的基本政策，坚持创新、协调、绿色、开放、共享的发展理念，加快推进新型领域安全能力建设，为维护国家安全利益、和平利用新型领域提供重要支撑。近年来，中国积极参与新型领域的国际安全治理，为造福人类作出了重要贡献。

Protection of National Interests in the New Domains

New security domains are the areas entailing emerging security concerns, such as space, internet, AI, and biotechnology. They are distinguishable from traditional security areas and represent the development of security issues in our time. While they are the most dynamic areas of technological development on which humanity's future depends, efforts must be made to ward off and counter the potential threats to national security. It is essential in this respect to join global efforts for shared development, use, and management of technologies in the new security domains.

Guided by a vision for development that benefits all and emphasizes innovation, coordination, environmental protection, and openness, China will continue to build capacity in new and emerging areas to protect its national interests from any potential threat and support peaceful use of new technologies.

China's active participation in global security governance in the new domains in recent years has contributed significantly to the wellbeing of humanity.

海外利益攸关区

海外利益攸关区是指与海外利益存在客观密切联系的区域。2015年5月，中国发表《中国的军事战略》白皮书，提出“海外利益攸关区”概念。随着中国国家利益的拓展，维护海外利益安全已经成为军事战略高度关注的重要问题。在中国不断扩大全方位对外开放的过程中，中国海外能源资源、战略通道安全和海外机构、人员、资产安全问题日益凸显，开展海上护航、撤离海外公民、应急救援等海外行动和海外利益攸关区安全合作，成为中国军队维护国家利益和履行国际义务的重要方式。维护中国海外利益，是全球化时代保障国家可持续发展的需要，也有利于维护世界和地区安全稳定。中国的海外利益攸关区没有排他性和对抗性，不谋求划分势力范围和军事扩张。

Areas Crucial to China's Overseas Interests

The concept of areas crucial to China's overseas interests was laid out in the 2015 white paper *China's Military Strategy*. With China's growing global involvement, protection of overseas interests has become an important issue that should be dealt with as part of China's military strategy.

Increasing openness has led to increasing vulnerabilities for China's overseas interests, including energy resources, strategic passageways, China's overseas entities, assets, and nationals. Naval escorts, evacuation of overseas Chinese nationals, HADR operations, and cooperation in areas crucial to China's overseas interests have thus become an important part of the military's mission to protect national interests and fulfill China's international obligations.

Protection of China's interests abroad is key to ensuring sustained national development in a globalized world. It also contributes to world and regional security and stability. Cooperation in areas crucial to China's overseas interests is not intended to exclude or target anyone, nor is it an attempt to seek spheres of influence or pursue military expansion.

提供国际公共安全产品

军事领域的国际公共安全产品，主要是指国家或国家集团为谋求国际或地区安全稳定，而在世界或特定地区开展的维持和平行动、人道主义救援、海上护航，以及国际反恐怖行动、协助打击跨国犯罪等。中国始终坚定履行国际责任和义务，积极提供与国力相适应的国际公共安全产品。进入新时代，中国军队的影响力越来越广，提供的国际公共安全产品遍布全球。参与联合国维和行动，履行安理会授权，致力于和平解决冲突，促进发展和重建，维护地区和平与安全；积极参加国际灾难救援和人道主义援助，派遣专业救援力量赴受灾国救援减灾，提供救援物资与医疗救助，加强救援减灾国际交流；开展亚丁湾等海域的护航行动，加强与多国护航力量交流合作，共同维护国际海上通道

Public Security Goods Provided to the International Community

When it comes to military affairs, international public security goods refer to the efforts by one country or a group of countries to bolster international or regional security and stability through, *inter alia*, UN peacekeeping operations, HADR efforts, naval escorts, international counter-terrorism actions, and fight against transnational organized crimes. China is always committed to its international duties and obligations, and has done its part to contribute to global security.

The global influence of China's military in the new era grows with its expanding role in providing global public goods through:

- participation in UN peacekeeping operations authorized by the UN Security Council to resolve conflicts by peaceful means, promote development and reconstruction, and maintain regional peace and security;
- international HADR efforts by dispatching disaster response teams, participating in disaster reduction actions, providing disaster relief supplies and medical services, and bolstering international exchanges in disaster response and

安全；广泛参与地区和国际安全事务，推动建立突发情况通报、军事危险预防、危机冲突管控等机制。随着国力不断增强，中国军队将加大参与国际维和、国际人道主义救援等行动的力度，在力所能及范围内提供更多公共安全产品，为维护世界和平、促进共同发展作出更大贡献。

reduction;

- naval escorts in sea areas, including the Gulf of Aden and exchanges with other naval forces, to protect the security of international shipping; and
- extensive engagement in regional and international security issues and efforts to create necessary mechanisms for emergency notification, prevention of military risks, and crisis and conflict management.

With growing national strength, China's military will expand its participation in international engagements including UN peacekeeping and international HADR operations, and make a greater contribution to world peace and development.

参加联合国维和行动

中国积极支持联合国维和行动，是联合国维和行动的主要出资国之一，是安理会常任理事国中第一大出兵国。截至2020年9月，中国军队已累计参加25项联合国维和行动，派出维和军事人员4万余人次，16名中国军人牺牲在维和一线。中国军队在维和任务区新建、修复道路1.7万余千米，排除地雷及各类未爆物1.4万余枚；运送物资120万余吨，运输总里程1300万余千米；接诊救治病人、抢救伤员24.6万余人次；完成武装护卫、长短途巡逻等任务450余次。

2015年9月，中国加入新的联合国维和能力待命机制，建设8000人规模维和待命部队。2017年9月，中国完成维和待命部队在联合国的一级待命注册工作。2018年10月，13支分队高标准通过联合国组织

Participation in UN Peacekeeping Operations

China actively participates in UN peacekeeping operations, and is the largest troop-contributing country among the permanent members of the Security Council as well as a major financial contributor.

As of September 2020, China had participated in 25 UN peacekeeping missions, involving a total of over 40,000 Chinese military peacekeepers and costing 16 lives of Chinese service members. Activities undertaken by China's military in mission areas include the building or repairs of roads, totaling 17,000 kilometers in length; removal of more than 14,000 landmines and unexploded ordinance devices; transportation of 1.2 million tons of supplies, covering a total distance of 13 million kilometers; medical care and rescue provided for more than 246,000 people; and conduct of more than 450 armed escorts and patrols.

China joined the UN Peacekeeping Capability Readiness System (UNPCRS) in September 2015 and now has in place an 8,000-strong standby force of UN peacekeepers. The acceptance process at Level 1 for the standby units was completed in September 2017; 13 units were elevated to Level 2 in October 2018 after an assessment

的考核评估，晋升至二级待命状态。2019年至2020年，联合国将上述13支二级待命状态分队中的6支分队提升至三级待命状态。中国积极为各国培训维和人员，截至2020年9月已经为60多个国家培训了1500余名维和人员。2020年8月，2521名中国官兵正在8个维和特派团和联合国总部执行任务。

and advisory visit from the UN; and six of these 13 units were elevated to Level 3 in 2019 and 2020.

China had trained more than 1,500 peacekeepers from more than 60 countries by September 2020. The statistics of August 2020 showed that 2,521 PLA officers and soldiers were deployed in eight UN peacekeeping missions as well as in the UN headquarters.

亚丁湾护航

亚丁湾是连接包括中国在内的东亚国家和西欧及北美东海岸的重要航线，又是波斯湾石油输往欧洲和北美洲的重要水路。中国根据联合国安理会有关决议的安排和索马里过渡政府的请求，自2008年以来，截至2019年11月，累计向亚丁湾海域派出33批护航编队、106艘次舰艇、71架次直升机、2.7万余人次官兵，为6600余艘中外船舶护航，展现了中国负责任大国的担当。护航期间，中国海军护航官兵与各国海军密切合作，严格遵守国际法有关规定和联合国有关决议，积极为外国商船提供应急救援。在中国海军安全护送的船舶中，一半以上是外国船舶。中国海军护航编队先后与俄罗斯、美国等20余个国家护航舰艇开展联合护航、演练、交流与合作，还执行了马航失联航班搜救、为马尔代夫提供淡水等紧急任务，派舰前往地

Escort Missions in the Gulf of Aden

The Gulf of Aden is an important shipping route connecting East Asia – including China – with Western Europe and the east coast of North America, and a vital waterway for Persian Gulf oil shipped to Europe and North America.

As a responsible member of the international community, China dispatched its escort fleet on 33 sailings between 2008 and November 2019, involving a total of 106 warships, 71 helicopters and 27,000 service members, providing escorts for 6,600 Chinese and foreign vessels, in accordance with relevant UN Security Council resolutions and at the request of the Transitional Federal Government of Somalia.

China's fleet conducts escort missions in close coordination with other navies and in strict compliance with international law and UN resolutions, and provides emergency assistance to foreign merchant vessels when necessary. Over half of the vessels escorted were foreign vessels.

China's fleet has also conducted joint escort missions, joint exercises, and exchanges with more than 20 other escort fleets, including those from Russia and the US. Other activities include participation in the search for the missing Malaysian Airlines

中海对撤离利比亚中国公民的船舶实施护航，前往战火纷飞的也门港口成功将621名中国公民和来自15个国家的279名外国公民安全撤离。

plane, emergency delivery of freshwater to the Maldives, escort missions for vessels carrying Chinese citizens evacuated from Libya, and the safe evacuation of 621 Chinese citizens and 279 nationals of 15 countries from a Yemen port where fighting was going on.

“和谐使命”系列任务

“和谐使命”系列任务是中国主导的国际人道主义医疗救援行动。海军“和平方舟”医院船是中国自行设计建造的第一艘制式远洋医院船，排水量14300吨，设有伤病员换乘、检伤分类、门诊、住院、后送撤离五大医疗区，总面积4000平方米，被誉为海上“生命之舟”。自2010年以来，截至2019年11月，先后7次远赴海外执行任务，访问43个国家和地区，累计航程24万余海里，免费接诊病患23万余人次，在太平洋、印度洋、大西洋和亚洲、非洲、欧洲、大洋洲、北美洲、南美洲留下了中国“红十字”的身影和航迹。“和谐使命”系列任务，打造了国际医疗合作品牌，向世界传播了中国军队维护和平、关爱生命的真诚态度。

"Mission Harmony"

"Mission Harmony" is a series of Chinese-led international humanitarian actions in the form of medical services. China's naval hospital ship *Ark Peace* plays a prominent role in these missions.

With a displacement of 14,300 tons, the *Ark Peace* is the first ocean-going hospital ship of its kind specially designed and built by China. It has a total surface area of 4,000 square meters, and five zones for patient transfer, medical examination, outpatient care, hospitalization, and medical evacuation. It is often dubbed "the Ark of Life."

Between 2010 and November 2019, the ship undertook seven overseas missions across the Pacific, Indian and Atlantic oceans and visited 43 countries and regions in Asia, Africa, Europe, Oceania, North America, and South America, covering a distance of 240,000 nautical miles. It has provided free medical care to 230,000 people. "Mission Harmony" promotes international cooperation in medical services, and brings to the world the love of peace and the love of life.

驻吉布提保障基地

2017年8月1日（吉布提当地时间），中国人民解放军驻吉布提保障基地部队举行进驻营区仪式，这标志着中国首个海外保障基地建成和投入使用。这是中国军队为有效维护国家海外利益，更好地遂行海上护航、国际维和、国际人道主义救援、撤离海外中国公民等任务，在吉布提建立的保障基地。自开营以来，截至2019年7月，已为4批次护航编队保障维修器材，为百余名护航官兵提供医疗保障服务，同外军开展联合医疗救援演练等活动，并向当地学校捐赠600余件教学器材。

近年来，中国军队执行海上护航、国际维和、国际人道主义救援、撤离海外中国公民等任务越来越多，特别是2008年以来，根据联合国有关决议，中国已派出多批护航编队赴亚丁湾、索马里海域护航，在执行任务过程中，官兵休整和物资保障补给等面临着许多实际困难。中国在吉布

The PLA Djibouti Support Base

A ceremony was held on August 1, 2017 in Djibouti to mark the completion of China's first overseas support base and its entry into service with the deployment of the PLA units. The support base strengthens the ability of China's military to protect national interests abroad, conduct escort missions at sea, participate in UN peacekeeping operations and international humanitarian rescues, and evacuate Chinese nationals caught in emergencies.

By July 2019, personnel stationed there had provided maintenance and repair services for vessels participating in escort missions and medical services for over 100 sailors. They conducted joint medical relief exercises with foreign militaries, and donated 600 items of educational equipment to local schools.

Previously, growing overseas activities by China's military, including escort missions at sea, UN peacekeeping, international HADR operations, and evacuation of Chinese nationals, had difficulties in meeting logistics needs and arranging service members' layover stays. These inadequacies have been particularly prominent since 2008, when China dispatched escort fleets to the Gulf of Aden and waters off the coast of Somalia, in accordance with relevant UN resolutions.

提建立保障基地，是为了更好地履行负责任大国的国际责任和义务，提供国际公共安全产品，维护地区和平稳定，也有利于维护中国的合法权益。

The establishment of a support base in Djibouti enables China to better fulfill its duties and obligations as a responsible member of the international community, and better promote regional peace and stability, in addition to protecting China's legitimate interests.

北京香山论坛

北京香山论坛原称香山论坛，于2006年由中国军事科学学会发起，初为亚太地区安全“二轨”对话平台。论坛从2014年第5届起升级为“一轨半”，层级规模大幅提升，与会人员扩展为亚太地区和域外相关国家的国防部或军队领导人、国际组织代表、前军政要员及知名学者。自2015年第6届起，香山论坛由中国军事科学学会和中国国际战略学会共同主办。2018年第8届，更名为北京香山论坛。目前，北京香山论坛已发展成为具有重要国际影响力、开展国际安全和防务对话的重要平台。

论坛坚持开放、包容、互鉴、合作的理念，聚焦亚太地区乃至全球安全新形势、新机遇、新挑战，倡导平等对话、互利合作、共同安全，致力于集聚智慧、扩大共识、增进互信，为增强安全对话与防务联系、促进地区和平稳定发挥积极作用。

Beijing Xiangshan Forum

The Beijing Xiangshan Forum, formerly known as the Xiangshan Forum, was launched by the China Association of Military Sciences (CAMS) in 2006 as a "track 2" platform for Asia-Pacific security dialog. It was upgraded to the "track 1.5" status as of the Fifth Forum in 2014 with a wider spectrum of participants, including defense and military leaders, representatives of international organizations, former government officials, retired senior officers, and renowned academics from within the Asia-Pacific region and beyond.

Since the Sixth Forum in 2015, it has been co-hosted by the CAMS and the China Institute of International Strategic Studies (CIISS), and was renamed the Beijing Xiangshan Forum at its Eighth Forum in 2018. It has developed into an important platform for international dialog on security and defense issues, attracting global attention.

Bearing in mind the importance of openness, inclusiveness, mutual learning and cooperation, the Forum is committed to serving as a platform for exchanging ideas, expanding consensus, building mutual trust, and bolstering regional security. It benefits all through dialog on the basis of equality with a focus on new global and regional security trends, new opportunities and new

2019年10月20日至22日，第9届北京香山论坛在北京国际会议中心举行，76个官方代表团、23国国防部长、6国军队总长（国防军司令）、8个国际组织代表及专家学者和各国观察员等1300余名嘉宾出席，围绕“维护国际秩序，共筑亚太和平”主题展开了多场研讨。

challenges.

The Ninth Forum was convened at the Beijing International Convention Center from October 20 to 22, 2019, with the attendance of more than 1,300 people, including 76 official delegations, 23 defense ministers, six chiefs of staff and representatives of eight international organizations, as well as academics and observers from different countries, and a wide range of topics discussed on the theme of "Maintaining International Order and Promoting Peace in the Asia-Pacific."

图书在版编目（CIP）数据

中国军事关键词：汉英对照 / 中国外文出版发行事业局，当代中国与世界研究院，中国翻译研究院著；蔡力坚译 . -- 北京：新世界出版社，2021.1
ISBN 978-7-5104-7234-3

Ⅰ . ①中… Ⅱ . ①中… ②当… ③中… ④蔡… Ⅲ . ①国防建设－概况－中国－汉、英②军队建设－概况－中国－汉、英 Ⅳ . ① E2

中国版本图书馆 CIP 数据核字 (2021) 第 009385 号

中国军事关键词（汉英对照）

作　　者：中国外文出版发行事业局　当代中国与世界研究院
　　　　　中国翻译研究院
翻　　译：蔡力坚
审　　定：徐明强
审　　读：韩清月
改　　稿：David Ferguson [英]
责任编辑：孔德芳
特约编辑：申　阳　赵如意
责任印制：王宝根
出版发行：新世界出版社
社　　址：北京西城区百万庄大街 24 号（100037）
发 行 部：(010) 6899 5968 (010) 6899 8705（传真）
总 编 室：(010) 6899 5424 (010) 6832 6679（传真）
http://www.nwp.cn　http://www.nwp.com.cn
版 权 部：+8610 6899 6306
版权部电子信箱：nwpcd@sina.com
印　　刷：天津旭非印刷有限公司
经　　销：新华书店
开　　本：880mm × 1230mm　1/32
字　　数：100 千字　　印　　张：7.875
版　　次：2021 年 1 月第 1 版　2021 年 1 月第 1 次印刷
书　　号：ISBN 978-7-5104-7234-3
定　　价：68.00 元